The Open University

D103 SOCIETY AND SOCIAL SCIENCE: A FOUNDATION COURSE

BLOCK 6
THE MAKING OF THE REGIONS

THE OPEN UNIVERSITY

D103 PRODUCTION TEAM

John Allen
James Anderson (Chairperson)
Robert Bocock
Peter Bradshaw
Vivienne Brown
Linda Clark (Course Secretary)
David Coates
Allan Cochrane
Jeremy Cooper (BBC)
Neil Costello
Clare Falkner (BBC)
Stuart Hall
Susan Himmelweit
Jack Leathem (BBC)
Richard Maidment
Doreen Massey
Gregor McLennan
Andrew Northedge
Kay Pole
Marilyn Ricci (Course Manager)
Paul Smith
Richard Stevens
Elaine Storkey
Kenneth Thompson
Diane Watson
Margaret Wetherell

External Consultants
Tom Burden
David Deacon
David Denver
Caroline Dumonteil
Owen Hartley
Tom Hulley
Robert Looker
Angela Phillips
Colm Regan
Richard Sanders
Neil Thompson
Patrick Wright

Tutor Assessors
Alan Brown
Lyn Brennan
Mona Clark
Ian Crosher
Donna Dickenson
Brian Graham
Philip Markey
Norma Sherrat
Jan Vance

Tom Hunter, Chris Wooldridge, David Wilson, Robert Cookson, Nigel Draper, David Scott-Macnab (Editors); Paul Smith (Librarian); Alison George (Graphic Artist); Jane Sheppard (Designer); Sue Rippon, Mollie Hancock (Project Control); Robin Thornton (Summer School Manager); John Hunt (Summer School IT); John Bennett; and others.

External Academic Assessors
Professor Anthony Giddens, Cambridge University (Overall Assessor)
Dr Geoffrey Harcourt, Cambridge University (Block III)
Dr Patrick Dunleavy, London School of Economics (Block IV)
Dr Hella Beloff, Edinburgh University (Block V)
Professor Brian Robson, Manchester University (Block VI)

The Open University,
Walton Hall, Milton Keynes,
MK7 6AA.

First Published 1991. Reprinted 1992, 1993, 1994. Copyright © 1991 The Open University

Designed by the Graphic Design Group of The Open University.

Typeset by The Open University and printed in the United Kingdom by The Alden Press, Oxford.

ISBN 0 7492 0042 1

For general availability of supporting material referred to in this text, please write to Open University Educational Enterprises Limited, 12 Cofferidge Close, Stony Stratford, Milton Keynes, MK11 1BY, United Kingdom.

Further information on Open University courses may be obtained from the Admissions Office, The Open University, P.O. Box 48, Walton Hall, Milton Keynes, MK7 6AB.

1.4

BLOCK INTRODUCTION AND STUDY GUIDE

Prepared for the Course Team by John Allen

CONTENTS

1 THE STORY SO FAR

In each of the previous blocks you were introduced to a different dimension of how the modern UK has been put together — how the UK has been made, or more accurately, remade over time. Each block addressed a different set of issues, some located within a global context and others presented within a historical context. In doing so, each block added something to the overall storyline of why the UK today is like the way that it is. Each block, may be read as a separate chapter of that 'story', although a richer understanding of how a society is put together can perhaps best be grasped by tracing the social relations that connect the different blocks.

Take an example from early on in the course, from Block II in fact, that of social class. If we wish to build up a comprehensive picture of the contemporary class structure in the UK, then, with the benefit of hindsight, we would need to consider many of the economic changes discussed in Block III, especially those concerned with the shifts in the nature of industry — from manufacturing to services, for example — and the changes in the nature of work and the types of jobs on offer, and for whom. Moreover, we would need to go beyond the economic connections. We would need also to think about the political and the cultural links raised in Blocks IV and V respectively. From Block IV, we may wish to consider what role, if any, the state has played in altering the class structure and class inequalities in the contemporary UK. To what extent, for example, have state policies transformed the UK's manufacturing base or the public provision of welfare? And from Block V, any concern with the remaking of classes inevitably leads us to consider questions of changing cultural identities and what it means today, to think of oneself as say, working class or upper middle class.

Class is, of course, only one kind of social relationship that can be traced through D103 in this way. It represents one point of entry into the course storyline and it possesses its own distinctive track through the units. If you are black and British, how the UK has been remade in the post-war period will very likely represent a quite different, yet overlapping 'story'. How the UK has been made and remade over time — economically, politically, culturally — affects us all, but in quite different ways. In this block, we want to take this approach a step further. We want to show that the making of the modern UK is a 'story' not just with many parts and a variety of actors, ranging from individuals to supra-national institutions, but a 'story' that varies dramatically from one part of the country to another. You will certainly be aware of this fact from the television series. Here we intend to examine why national changes rarely, if ever, take a unified or single form; why national changes work themselves out unevenly across the country and affect our lives in diverse ways. In recent years the social geography of the UK has altered considerably, and it is the nature of these changes and how they have affected the overall direction of change in UK society that this block sets out to explore and explain.

2 WHY STUDY THE GEOGRAPHY OF SOCIETY?

If the UK is changing in different ways across the country, then the very fact of difference means that it is a worthwhile topic of study. If whole regions in the north of the country are changing in ways that are quite different from those in the south and if the fortunes of some cities are benefitting from the national shift to services whilst other cities find their manufacturing core reduced to wasteland and dereliction, then the difference deeply affects peoples' lives in those areas. If, for example, the decline of the manufacturing working class is not happening in the same way across the country, then its uneven geography is part and parcel of the way in which classes are being remade in the UK. The outer estates of Liverpool or of Glasgow represent a different set of life chances, as well as a very different kind of place, from say the suburbs of Oxford or the gentrified streets of inner London. The differences influence our day-to-day lives and set the context in which we live them.

All of this means that, as you will have probably realized, we are not concerned with the differences between places simply for their own sake. The differences actually matter *socially* in a variety of ways.

At a very broad level, for instance, the geography of society is at one and the same time a geography of inequality. The division between the north and south of the UK, the differences between the regions, and the city-country divide are each in their own way about differences in economic fortune. The growth of the new industries, for example, is not happening in the same place as the decline of the old. Moreover, some cities and regions have experienced growth on top of growth, new jobs on top of plenty. At the same time, other places have been left behind or sidestepped by the new dynamics of industrial growth, even within the 'prosperous' regions. In fact, what this adds up to is a process of uneven economic development across the country. And, as we shall see later in the block, this geographical unevenness carries with it a series of obstacles for the economic development of the nation as a whole and its social and political cohesion.

When we talk about space making a difference therefore, we are not just referring to the different dynamics of economic growth underway across the country. People live out their lives in different parts of the country, shaped in part by broader political and cultural processes which also possess an uneven geography. Again, at a very general level, it is possible to map the contours of cultural change and to show how new cultural forms cut across the old. In some of the big cities, for example, the decline of a 'traditional' working class culture and a distinctive work-place politics based on the trade unions has taken place alongside the growth of an enterprise culture and a politics centred on the individual. The two cultures co-exist uneasily, and just as certain parts of the country have become associated with fixed yet outdated cultural traits (the hard, cloth-capped male breadwinner in the north and the soft, southerner), so the new forms find their social base in different locations. Old cultural patterns slide into new ones in parts of the south east, while a process of resistance and negotiation slows the pace of cultural change elsewhere. In part, local and regional politics draw their strength from such cultural differences and at a broader spatial scale they are reflected in, for example, the rise of nationalist politics in Scotland and Wales.

Pulling all this together gives you some idea of the broad aim of the block, which is to examine and explain the nature of *uneven development* in the UK, and why it matters.

To convey something of the full richness of uneven development in the U.K. we will examine the country's changing geography in two ways:

First, we will explore aspects of all three dimensions of uneven development in the UK, starting with the cultural and moving on to the economic and then the political. We will also briefly consider the different pace of change associated with each dimension and illustrate how they combine in different ways in different places.

Second, we will explore the changing geography of the UK through the lens as it were of the local-global theme. In one sense, the study of uneven development is inseparable from the study of the *links* between a local area and the wider context of which it is a part. Whether the local refers to Wigan or to the UK, the *links* of both areas to the wider context — the 'global' — is central to an understanding of what is happening in those places and, indeed, they may well tell us something about changes at the 'global' level too.

3 THE ORGANIZATION OF THE BLOCK

The block therefore takes its cue from the local-global theme. Indeed, aspects of the theme will be familiar to you. You may remember, for example, how Unit 1 gave us a sense of how the rest of the world is already part of the UK and how it has helped to shape our cities and regions for the best part of two hundred years. But what does it actually mean to say that global processes are an integral part of the changing fortunes of the UK and its cities and regions? For one thing, it does not mean that what happens in the UK is merely a reflection of world events, as if developments across the country are simply a response to more powerful, global pressures. There is far more to it than that. There is a sense in which the local and the global *cross-cut* one another to generate patterns of uneven development in the UK. In other words there is an *interaction* between wider national and international processes and the peculiarities of place that make say, the North East a distinctive region or Liverpool a unique place with a unique character. In this block we have tried to convey this sense of place and the uneven nature of the UK's development by organizing the units around the local-global connection. In doing so, we have focused upon developments over the last two centuries, drawing out the importance of certain historical periods — such as the 'Age of Empire' in the nineteenth century and the contemporary post-war period — which were crucial to changes in the UK's fortunes and its regions.

Unit 23 starts the geographical 'story' by unravelling the threads of global influence that make up the local character of places. Using the example of Lancashire, the unit shows how industry in Lancashire in the heyday of cotton nearly two centuries ago was as much a part of the world economy as Manchester is in the 1990s. That is not to say however, that the same kinds of relationships hold today between the local and the global. The days of the Empire and Britain's Imperial dominance have passed and in their place a new kind of global presence is felt. Today, for example, multinationals criss-cross the globe, joining places together in new ways and forging new forms of interdependent relationships, cultural as well as economic.

If Unit 23 looks *outwards* from the local to the global, then Unit 24 looks *inwards*, as it were, to explore the changing economic fortunes of cities and regions within the post-war UK. This is a Britain which has all but lost its 'workshop of the world' tag; a Britain of different regional divides and inequalities that reflect the diversity of its global links in services and in manufacturing. Moreover, it is a Britain that politically, has lost the status of a leading world power. Unit 25 picks up this political progression and moves it *out* again, placing the local in the global, although this time within the framework of the recent developments that have remade Europe. It explores the thesis set up in Unit 23 which suggests that if the traditional industrial regions based on heavy industry have declined along with the UK and its Empire, we are now witnessing a new kind of integration of the regions within a much wider European political and economic system.

Unit 26 has a different role to play within the block. Whereas the first three units of the block examine aspects of the cultural, economic, and political dimensions of uneven development in the UK, Unit 26 performs a review role. As part of a cumulative sequence of review units associated with each block it is concerned with the nature of social science enquiry and in this case, it reviews Block VI through an examination of how we make choices between competing explanations.

4   STUDYING THE BLOCK.

As you work your way through Block VI you will, as with previous blocks, be asked to read selected articles from the Reader and make notes on the associated television and radio programmes. The detailed instructions on how to use this bundle of materials are in the unit texts and the *Media Booklet*. Here, very briefly, we want to comment on the relationship of the various course components to the ideas developed in the units and to give you a sense of how the block as a whole is organized.

4.1   TELEVISION, RADIO AND AUDIO-CASSETTE

The block is accompanied by two television programmes, three radio slots, and one audio-cassette. The two television programmes perform a particular role within the block. In different ways, they are intended to develop and to highlight the interconnections between local-global relations. TV 12 is closely connected with the aims of Unit 23 in so far as the programme shows how the internationalization of the UK economy over the last century has affected regional economies in different ways, with the fortunes of the North East and the South East, for example, changing in response to a changed world economic order. A similar line of enquiry is constructed in TV13, although this time it takes its brief from Unit 25. This programme sets local politics within a wider European framework. With the help of case studies from the UK and France, it considers the extent to which internationalization has made it possible for localities to develop their own economic initiatives. And it goes further to look at some of the ways in which localities and regions build links to each other and to the political system represented by the European Community, possibly bypassing existing structures of national government.

The European dimension is also explored in the second of the three radio programmes, although here the emphasis is upon future developments in Europe and their potential economic and political implications for the direction of the UK and its cities and regions. The first radio slot is somewhat different in so far as it addresses the summar school experience. This includes issues related to Block VI, as well as to Blocks V and VII. The final radio programme occupies the familiar 'Assignment–103' slot.

The audio-cassette performs a different role from that of the television and the radio programmes. Its role is to consolidate some of the main ideas raised in the block and, where appropriate, to draw out and to strengthen some of the connections between issues discussed in the units.

4.2   COURSE READER

The block has three Reader chapters associated with it, one for each of the three units. Chapter 19, *Global Local Times* acts as an overview of contemporary developments in the globalization of economic and cultural forms and stresses the importance of the local in a world that today, tends to emphasize blanket global trends. Chapters 20 and 21, on Swindon and Middlesborough respectively, are drawn from a recent collection of locality studies. In both cases, the detailed changes within those areas are explained within a wider, global context. If you choose to answer the TMA option on your local area you will find that each of the three chapters has something to offer. Further details of this option are set out in your *TMA Booklet*.

4.3   RESOURCE FILE

If you do intend to answer the TMA option on your local area, you will also find it useful to compile a cuttings file on your locality. Obviously, there is a danger here of collecting far too much information and we suggest that you focus on two aspects of your locality. First, think about some of the more recent changes in your area and follow them up in local (and possibly national) newspapers or perhaps jot down ideas from local television and radio programmes. The sorts of changes noted can be of any kind: economic, political or cultural. Second, once you have picked out some of the changes in your area which interest you, you could take your research a step further by collecting information on how they *may* be related to national and possibly international changes. So, for example, have recent or past national government policies had a particular impact on your area? Or have important political or economic events elsewhere in the world had a direct bearing on the economic fortunes of your own town or city? These are the sorts of 'leads' you may wish to follow. Even if you decide not to answer the TMA option on your local area, you may well find that the resources that you have collected will give you an insight into some of the issues and arguments discussed in the block.

4.4   SUMMER SCHOOL

Many of you will be studying this block while at the D103 Summer School and others will have the Summer School as a memory only. For those of you who have yet to go, one of the three summer school modules, 'Making the Environment', takes up and extends the account of uneven development introduced in this block. Growth and the environment are key aspects of the module; aspects which are developed along the cultural, economic and political lines of the block as a whole. Many of the ideas which are introduced in the module ask you to reflect upon and perhaps reconsider conventional ways of thinking about economic growth and development. In this way, the module represents another strand of geographical thought and one that adds further insight into changing local-global relations.

4.5   SUGGESTED STUDY PROGRAMME

Block components	Approximate Study Time (Hours)
Block Introduction and Study Guide	$\frac{1}{2}$
Unit 23: A Global Sense of Place	$6\frac{1}{2}$
Reader: Chapter 19	2
Radio 11	$\frac{1}{2}$
Tape 6	1
Total	$10\frac{1}{2}$
Unit 24: Uneven development and regional inequality	$6\frac{1}{2}$
Reader: Chapter 20	3
TV 12 'Regions Apart' (and *D103 Media Booklet*)	2
Total	$11\frac{1}{2}$
Unit 25: From United Kingdom to United Europe?	$6\frac{1}{2}$
Study Skills Section: How are you progressing?	$\frac{1}{2}$
Reader: Chapter 21	$2\frac{1}{2}$
The Good Study Guide: Chapter 7, Sections 1 and 2	1
Radio 12	$\frac{1}{2}$
Total	11
Unit 26: Choosing between explanations	$3\frac{1}{2}$
TV 13 'A Europe of the Regions' (and *D103 Media Booklet*)	2
Radio 13	$\frac{1}{2}$
TMA 06	6
Total	12

UNIT 23   A GLOBAL SENSE OF PLACE

Prepared for the Course Team by Doreen Massey

CONTENTS

1   INTRODUCTION

Our subject-matter in this block revolves around a number of basic geographical terms — terms such as space, place and uneven development. 'Geography' these days is about a lot more than mountains and rivers! This unit sets out to give you a flavour of it, and to introduce you to some of the basic concepts in a number of wide-ranging debates. The biggest single debate which runs through the unit revolves around the apparently simple question: What is a place? The first part of the unit explores how we think about places, and how we often partly identify ourselves with them. It also looks at some of the cultural ways in which regions and areas differ from each other. Later parts of the unit focus more on the economic and employment aspects of uneven development. Running through this debate is the important point that while we can all recognize (or think we can recognize) the local character of a place, we can also see in it signs of its links to an international economy, to international communications systems, and to threads of dominant world cultures.

In this unit, then, we discuss variations within the UK itself. Although in much of the course so far we have talked about the UK as a whole, it has also been clear that there is great differentiation between one place and another. An important focus of this unit is to examine how different places within this country (a region, for example, or a local area) relate to the wider context in which they are set. In the local–global theme of the course there is a strong argument that we cannot understand places without understanding the links they have with other areas. In *Section 3* of this unit, we examine some case-studies (Lancashire, south Wales and central Scotland) in order to explore this proposition in more detail. Building on this, *Section 4* presents a brief historical survey of uneven development in the UK, emphasizing the relation between the economic fortunes of different regions and their links to the international economy. The local and regional identities of different parts of the UK, in that sense, have for a long time been influenced by international factors.

The fact that such identities are important was indicated in Block V. As you saw there, people answering the questionnaire on identity might well respond by saying 'I'm a Scot' or 'a Northerner' or 'a Cockney'. In answering in this way they are drawing on representations of places which they expect others to share, or at least to understand. Yet representations of places may in fact vary between different groups, even between those living in the same area. What, then, *is* a place? It is with an exploration of that issue that *Section 2* of this unit is concerned.

2   PLACES

Even within an area as small as the United Kingdom, different places have distinct images. What do you think of when you think of Yorkshire or Liverpool, Mayfair or the Welsh Valleys, or the Highlands of Scotland? Such images extend from the natural or physical environment, through economy and social structure, to culture. Yorkshire people — so the stereotype runs — are tightfisted, Liverpudlians are always having a laugh, the people of the valleys of south Wales live lives closely tied around rugby, singing in choirs, and a highly disciplined labour movement.

But I could just as easily write a paragraph arguing almost the opposite point of view…

Places are all the same these days. They are losing their individuality. Every major city centre has its big, modern buildings and almost every city centre has its concrete shopping arcade with the same pedestrian precincts, outlets of the same range of shops, same escalators and the same environmentally-insensitive plants. If you were magically transported to the middle of one of them you might well be hard put to decide which town you were in. You can even say the same thing internationally. The airports are indistinguishable, and you can always find a McDonalds and a Coca Cola.

What do you make of these two different positions? *Do* places have their own local character?

One fairly immediate response you might have, and which I certainly find is reflected in the paragraphs I have written above, is that the individuality of places is a product of their *past* character but that they are *now* coming to look alike. The distinctiveness of parts of the country and parts of the world is thus a product of their *historical* association, perhaps with particular economies, perhaps based on local resources or advantages, and on local cultures. But the Lancashire economy no longer has its distinctive basis in cotton, almost all the coal mines in south Wales have been closed, Clydeside can no longer so easily be identified with ships, and whatever happened to the linen industry of Northern Ireland? And yet there *are* continuities. Perhaps the most enduring fact of British economic geography is the centuries-long identification of a small part of London with finance, merchanting, insurance and the like.

Perhaps this historically-derived geographical distinctiveness is something which the spread of international capitalism, new technology and modernity has been rapidly eradicating. Maybe it is in a reaction to this (as well as out of a need to create more jobs) that the 'heritage industry' has grown so dramatically in recent years. Is York proclaiming its Viking forebears as a way of reclaiming the past and rejecting the impetus towards a geographical sameness? Is it a way of trying to establish a 'local identity'? (Yet the move towards 'designer cities', the transformation for instance of previously run-down working class or industrial parts of inner urban areas into havens for expensive town-houses and up-market boutiques, or the gentrification of 'rural' villages, also often result in homogeneity. If you were to parachute into one of these new 'waterfront developments', as with airports and shopping centres, you'd be hard put to know where you were. Is it Cardiff, or Salford, or Bristol?)

Or perhaps, as ever, the issue is more complicated. Perhaps places are indeed retaining some form of individuality, but within an increasingly internationalized context where the difference derives not only from centuries-old (supposedly) historical roots but from that locality's own particular amalgam of those roots with internationally-derived influences and connections. Perhaps, in other words, *both* my opening paragraphs are true: there is *both* distinctiveness *and* similarity, and a real tension between them. And so we have the Japanization of Sunderland (you will look at this in TV12), and yet it is very clearly Sunderland. There are companies from all over the world in Corby but the place is still also clearly a town in middle England recently built, a town built for steel, and where a Scottish accent still occasionally sounds in the streets, an echo of the fact that the steel workers were transferred down here when their own steel industry went into decline, only to have been made redundant again when Corby too was closed. So now the Scots people of Corby, Northamptonshire, may work in companies which have links to the USA, Germany, the Netherlands, Finland, Sweden, France, Denmark, Australia, Spain, Switzerland, South Africa, Japan or China! Even the Square Mile of 'the City' of London, which has lasted for so long, has been challenged (as you will also see in TV12). Its old elitist customs of gentlemen's agreements, finishing work after (a good) lunch and shooting each other's grouse at the weekend, where a gentleman's word is his bond, has been blown apart by the arrival of US and Japanese banks with endless open-plan dealing floors and as many videoscreens as people ... yet it is still indisputably 'the City'.

Luxury housing, Ocean Village, Southampton

In these opening paragraphs we have already set out for further exploration three ideas about places:

- *first*, the idea that places seem to share more and more in common, yet still retain their individuality;

- *second*, the idea that there may be a relation between the character of places and their past histories;

- *third*, the idea that this local character is embedded in — and indeed partly made up of — links to the wider world, including the international world.

We shall continue to follow these ideas as we go through the unit. And indeed it is the last idea which is the key to our whole argument and which gives rise to the title of the unit: *A Global Sense of Place*.

─────────────── ACTIVITY I ───────────────

Try thinking through the above ideas in relation to a place that you know. (If you are going to do the TMA on your local area and its wider links, this would be a good time to start thinking about it.) Look for signs of the past and for links with the world beyond the local area.

I sat in a cafe on the front in a small south-coast seaside resort not so long ago. People pulled their cardigans tightly around them against the wind (it was high summer!), there were fishing boats pulled up on the steep slope of the beach before me, and a castle on a towering chalk mound; there were fish and chip shops selling local fish. There were also 'shoppes' selling cream teas (yet Devon and Cornwall are at least 150 miles to the west); there were Chinese takeaways, there was even a Chinese fish-and-chip shop. Stalls and shops sold articles and 'souvenirs' made anywhere and everywhere, from virtually down the road to the far east of Asia. A family walked by, the women wearing saris underneath their cardigans, the children trailing buckets and spades. Up the road were offices and factories of foreign-owned companies, to which 'the locals' would return on Monday morning.

So what is 'local culture' here?

One student of local cultures has written that 'One no longer leaves home confident of finding something radically new, another time or space. Difference is encountered in the adjoining neighbourhood, the familiar turns up at the ends of the earth' (Clifford, 1988, p.11, cited in Gregory and Ley, 1988, p.116).

Don't just rush on. Think about that last quotation. There are ancient advertisements for Andrews Liver Salts in one-horse towns in the Mexican desert and there's a C & A in Rio behind Copacabana beach. What elements from other places can you identify in your own neighbourhood, and yet which are part of the place?

So what are we to make of it all?

2.1   REPRESENTATIONS OF PLACES

'Do places have their own local character?', we asked in the last section. In order to come to grips with a question like this, we must pull it apart and address different aspects of it separately. In this section we shall examine one of the key terms in the question — *local character*.

This immediately raises one of the themes of the course. Before we go any further, we must be clear that the local characteristics which are attributed to places are images. They are not in some sense the places themselves; they are *representations* of them. And as representations they therefore have to be constructed.

New housing, Atlantic Wharf, East Dock, Cardiff

One clear indication of this is that there can be different and sometimes radically conflicting representations of the same place. Let's look at an example. Below I have reproduced three passages from a book by Patrick Wright (1985) (you met him in TV03). Each passage describes a particular image of Hackney, an inner-city borough in the eastern part of London. In spite of being registered as being the 'poorest borough in Britain' in at least one report (Wright, p.231), there is much social change going on in Hackney.

The first image is that held by the long-established white working class, a group which has its own 'sense of the area and its past' (ibid. p.232). For this group, 'the past' of Hackney focuses on the High Street...

> There are many older people who remember a more prosperous High Street as it was in the fifties — there was at least one large departmental store, and the pavements could be so crowded on Saturdays that people had to walk in the road. This remembered past exists in stark contrast with the present, for if the High Street is still the place to shop it has clearly also seen better days. A recently introduced one-way system drove some trade out of what is also an arterial road leading in the direction of Cambridge and other august locations ... The big department store was demolished — after years of dereliction — by the beginning of 1984, and many of the more recent shops (like Marks and Spencer) have relocated in the current economic decline. As for the large supermarkets of recent years (Sainsbury's, Safeway and so on), these have started as they mean to go on — elsewhere (p.232).

> Annette, a twenty one year old white woman ... finds it hard to believe that anyone would ever *choose* to live in this borough: she herself has eyes set on Kent or, failing that, Essex (p.235).

But, as well as the white working class, there are also ethnic-minority communities, which form a significant part of the Hackney population. This, then, is the second image:

> There is a long established Jewish population in the area with its Hasidic community concentrated slightly to the north of Stoke Newington in Stamford Hill. There are Irish, African, Italian, Asian, Cypriot (both Greek and Turkish) and West Indian people in the area — people who have their own routes through the place, although not necessarily ones that move in any easy accordance with the imaginative reconstructions and memories which hold the measure of the place for many white inhabitants. Given the prevailing white criteria, which measure belonging and cultural authenticity in terms of continuity of place and an imaginary valuation of the remaining trace, it is entirely consistent that the belonging for these people should seem (and I speak here from a dominant point of view) more makeshift and improvised. For people excluded from conventional identification with the area's historical geography, the traditional structure of the place is still there to be dealt with (p.234).

There has also, since the late 1960s, been gentrification — the middle class has been moving in. A third image, then, is held by this group:

> It enters the area with an attention of its own — with particular ways of appropriating the place in which it finds and must sustain and understand itself. Alongside the ethnic restaurants ... therefore, this is

also where a sense of the past comes in. Suddenly this hardpressed inner-city area is a settlement again — a new town in the wood as the name Stoke Newington would suggest to those interested in the historical meanings of place names. Because this upwardly mobile slum is in an old country, ... the new focus is certainly centred on Church Street, even though the commercial and retailing centres are firmly established elsewhere (on the more recession-struck High Street for example), and even though the old Borough of Stoke Newington has been integrated into the bigger administrative quagmire known as Hackney. Of course Church Street, being westerly, is just that little bit closer to respectable Highbury and further from the rather less gentrified wastes of Clapton and other places east. For this reason among others, perhaps it is not so surprising that a sense of local history should be making its way down to meet the newcomers along this particular road. This, after all, is the road in which the area's great names tend to congregate. Daniel Defoe lived on Church Street and Harriet Beecher Stowe stayed in a house at what used to be its junction with Carysfort Road; Isaac Watts wrote his hymns in a no longer existing mansion off to the north and as a young boy Edgar Allan Poe went to school at the connection with Edwards Lane. There is also the old Victorian Free Library in which this sort of information can be looked up, and eighteenth century 'Tall Houses', as they were known locally, survive on the south side of the road...

I'm not suggesting that these new settlers have exactly researched the history of the area, only that a certain appreciation of the remaining past has facilitated their settlement in the area ... So it happens that one of the several building societies opening branches in the area (often on the back of booming estate agents) fills its windows with eighteenth and nineteenth century images of the place.

(Wright, 1985, pp. 227-8)

New housing Mariners Canal, Salford Quays

I have cited these three quotations at some length because I now want you to work on them, to explore a bit further what is involved in 'images of place'.

But before you do that, we need to be clear about what kind of evidence this is that you are going to explore. Like all evidence it will need interpreting. Moreover, this is qualitative evidence about people's views. If we were really embarking on a piece of research we would want to enquire in detail about how Patrick Wright collected his evidence. He has obviously made generalizations: surely not all members of the white working class have exactly the same image of Hackney, for instance? (The debates about methodology in Block V would be relevant here.) Further, Wright is, as he himself remarks in the second quotation, speaking 'from a dominant point of view', and what we are reading is his interpretation (representation) of the views of others.

None of this invalidates his writing. It just means that we must bear these facts in mind when we, in turn, interpret the passages.

—————————————— ACTIVITY 2 ——————————————

Read through the passages again and note down:

1   What is each group's sense of the history of the place?
2   How is it related to their evaluation of the area now?
3   Do the groups even have the same geographical idea of the area?
4   Are the images just 'different', or are there potential or actual conflicts between them?

The groups clearly have different images of the borough, both past and present. Thus, to take up Questions 1 and 2 in the Activity, each group's interpretation of 'the past' influences their view of the place today. The white working class remembers a Hackney (not so long ago) which was more prosperous, with the shops on High Street full and busy. It is a remembered past which has been disrupted by decline (to a classic inner-city area of the 1980s and 1990s we may think), and those who have not already got out dream of leaving for the suburbs. For the middle class the past lies further back, predominantly in the seventeenth and eighteenth centuries when there was an intellectual community in the area. It is a past which is there, in buildings and street signs for instance, and only needs to be recovered and refurbished (the 'real' Hackney?) to enhance both their sense of living in a part of town 'with character' and the values of their property. The middle class, with the money to recover and refurbish, is moving in. Other incomers — over a much longer period — have been people from a variety of ethnic minority groups. Each of these is distinct, the Jewish population is 'long established', the other groups probably more recently-arrived, but each, according to this white English observer, is 'excluded from conventional identification with the area's historical geography'. What is clear from all this is that the notion of finding a locality's character 'in its past' is as problematical as finding it in the present. For although places may (or may not) have been more different from each other in the past, *defining that past involves interpretation*. This throws more light, then, on one of the ideas which were set up in the last section for further exploration. Certainly it may be true that there is a relation between the character of a place and its past history; but there is no single 'authentic' past. What 'eighteenth and nineteenth century images of the place' do you think the building society fills its windows with? Presumably not ones of the poverty and squalor which just as surely existed. But what is also clear is that there are also sharply contrasting views of the place today.

The different groups would also seem to have different geographical ideas, or 'mental maps', of Hackney. Firstly, they all live different sets of lives within one 'place', having their own distinct spatial foci, routes and networks. For the white working class the map of the borough is centred on the High Street. For the middle class, Church Street, Stoke Newington, is the core Hackney. The ethnic minority groups have their own distinct spatial bases, the Hasidic community in Stamford Hill, for instance, and each has its 'own routes through the place'. Later in the same paragraph, Wright describes how there is a Turkish mosque and community centre on the High Street. It is housed in a building which was once used as a cinema, but was originally built as an 'entertainment palace'. In what must seem today (now that it is a mosque) like a real irony, it has domes whose shape immediately brings to mind the near east. Yet their original design had nothing to do, directly, with Islam. Rather, the domes were presumably meant to add a hint of 'the exotic Orient' to a Saturday night out.

Secondly, even the same bits of Hackney have different meanings for each group. For the older white working class the former cinema (for that is what it is to them) holds memories of nights out in times gone by. For the Turkish population, the building holds links to places far from Hackney, to family and friends, perhaps to childhood, in Cyprus maybe, or a village on the Anatolian plateau, or in Istanbul. For them it brings to life a cultural map which inextricably links 'local and global', thoughts of the eastern Mediterranean while standing here in Hackney.

Hackney Mosque, converted from a cinema

As Wright comments 'People live in different worlds even though they share the same locality' (p.237). And this in turn throws further light on the discussion in the last section. There, we began to explore the idea that the 'local' character of places is partly made up of links to the wider world, including the international. Here, we see that those links to the wider world can include the interpretations which people bring even to the bricks and mortar of a building.

But, to turn now to the point in question in the Activity, it is evident that in a multitude of ways these very distinct representations of Hackney compete and conflict with each other. For both the middle class and the white working class the valued images of the borough hark back to a time before most of the ethnic minority communities arrived in the area. The bustling, thriving past looked back to by the white working class has in part been disrupted precisely by the arrival of other groups. And the imagery of the middle class goes back to times before those of the later dominance of working class culture — they would possibly have viewed it as loud and 'brash'.

> These tensions between different appropriations of the place are articulated around many different phenomena or issues. Thus, for example, middle class incomers value Abney Park cemetery precisely because it is overgrown and four-fifths wild — a good place for a Gothic stroll. A different view is taken by some working class people (far more likely to have relatives buried in the place), who find the unknown and neglected appearance of this nineteenth-century cemetery a mark of decay, and argue that it should definitely be tidied up (p.236).

So, any representation of an area is a product of interpretation, and in that sense there is no one unproblematically objective image. There may be numerous images. In the discussion of Hackney, the focus was on contrasts defined in relation to class and ethnic group. But other lines of division may produce other contrasts. Many analysts have pointed to the contrasting mental maps of Belfast held by members of the Catholic and Protestant communities in that city, for instance. And the difference between women's and men's views of a place is also likely to be particularly marked. The characterization of south Wales with which I began Section 2 of this unit — as 'closely tied around rugby, singing in choirs, and a highly disciplined labour movement' mainly reflects men's activities in the region. And the definition of a region is also likely often to be in terms of paid work — Clydesiders build ships, people in the west Midlands make cars — than other forms of activity. In part this is because such types of employment obviously vary between places, though recent research by feminist geographers has pointed to marked variations which exist also in gender relations and domestic labour. Nor is it necessarily even the paid jobs done by the highest percentage of the labour force which are used to define regions — there are probably more secretaries and typists than anything else in London but have you ever heard the city referred to as a 'secretarial-and-clerical area'?! No; typically it has been exporting sectors (exporting from the region) which have taken pride of place in regional economic imagery, and the only example I can think of which makes women central to regional definition is cotton in Lancashire (maybe you can think of others — at a smaller scale there is Nottingham and lace, Macclesfield and the silkworkers, Grimsby and fish processing, Dundee and its long history of spinning and weaving).

Important exporting sectors are of course likely to affect the lives of everyone in the region, and not just those who work in them. Women's lives have been deeply affected by the dominance of mining in south Wales, for instance. But women's cultural and mental maps are nonetheless likely to be quite distinct from those of men, less dominated by pit, rugby pitch and working-men's club. Men and women, then, may both have different definitions of regions and also know them through distinct reference-systems, different spaces and geographical networks.

Places may also have different representations applied to them from inside and outside. The southerner's view of the north of England (whether it is whippets and cloth caps, glorious countryside, or the area you have to go through to get to the Edinburgh Festival) is in general very different from that of the northerner. Inner-city areas where the poor are concentrated have often been viewed with alarm by middle classes and governments alike. Gareth Stedman Jones, writing about London at the end of the nineteenth century argued that

The poor districts became an immense *terra incognita* periodically mapped out by intrepid missionaries and explorers who catered to an insatiable middle-class demand for travellers' tales. These writers sometimes expressed apprehension about the large and anonymous proletarian areas of South London, but the most extensive and the most feared area was the East End, a huge city itself in all but name. In a typical description, Walter Besant observed:

> The population is greater than that of Berlin or Vienna, or St. Petersburg, or Philadelphia ... in the streets there are never seen any private carriages; there is no fashionable quarter ... one meets no ladies in the principal thoroughfare. People, shops, houses, conveyances — all together are stamped with the unmistakeable seal of the working class ... perhaps the strangest thing of all is this: in a city of two million people there are no hotels! That means, of course, that there are no visitors.
>
> (Stedman Jones, 1971, p.14, citing Besant, 1901, pp.7–9)

Such writing may seem extreme, but that kind of view of 'the inner city' can still be found today though it is perhaps more likely to be expressive of ethnic differences than of class. Writing of the violence which had broken out at the 1976 Notting Hill Carnival the *Daily Express* asked 'Are police, then, to keep a "low profile" in black areas of our own capital city?' (1 September 1976; cited in Jackson, 1988, p.219-20), thereby, argues Jackson, revealing its own map of 'our own' (implicitly white) capital city with (implicitly alien) 'black areas' within it. In a book whose title (*There ain't no black in the Union Jack*) refers precisely to that kind of attitude, Paul Gilroy discusses the so-called 'inner-city problem' in these terms. He points out how the uneven geography of economic growth and decline is related also to concentrations of particular ethnic groups. He argues that it may, therefore, become difficult to 'distinguish the subjectivity based around "race" from feelings of neighbourhood, region and locality'. But, as he points out, the experience of these local areas, and the interpretation put upon them, is likely to vary dramatically between black settlers and, for instance, 'the white racist for whom the presence of black neighbours becomes a symbol of urban degeneration' (Gilroy, 1987, p.37).

So there can be different representations of places. This recognition, now generally accepted, is already an advance over earlier positions within geography which saw landscapes and places as 'things out there' whose form and structure could be simply described. But can there be *any* variety of representations, with any content at all? Is *any* representation possible? Here there is debate among cultural geographers investigating images of landscape. For one school of thought, since the representation is the creation of the 'reader' of the landscape, its content is relatively unconstrained by the 'reality' of the place itself. In one example of this position, Edward Said (1979) argues that all those notions we in the UK hold, or have heard, of 'the mysterious Orient' are in fact the creation of a group of Western European Orientalists of a certain period. He argues that all those ideas of 'a place of romance, exotic beings, haunting memories and landscapes, remarkable experiences' (remember the old entertainment palace on Hackney High Street?) were almost a European invention. It was to Europeans that the images of the near east were 'romantic' and 'exotic'. But if Said is arguing that the representation may not be constrained by the 'place' itself, he is not arguing that it is completely random. In the case we are discussing here, he would argue that this view of 'the Orient' was a product of the needs of the currently-dominant European powers. (You will remember from TV10, in which Said appeared, that he discussed the political uses that representations can have.)

Representations of places, in this interpretation, while they are certainly not simple mirrors of 'the real place' do have to have some basis. They are, it is argued, the product of particular social experiences and they reflect specific value systems.

All this may seem to be becoming a bit ethereal. But in fact that is the last thing that it is. For representations matter. Dominant representations may reflect dominant value-systems and in turn serve to reinforce them. As was explained in Unit 17, the ability to persuade people that your representation is the correct one is an important source of power. Representations may have other effects, too. In a recent television discussion about images of Liverpool, Liverpudlians pointed out how the images which rely on nostalgia (how great it used to be living on 'the Scotty Road') are ultimately debilitating because they can rob people of any sense either of progress (it was *not* actually that great living on Scotland Road) or that things can be changed for the better in the future. They also pointed out that when some Liverpudlians play up to the stereotypical image, they 'are doing the classic thing that a colonialized people does', i.e., acquiescing in someone else's definition of them. Representations of places can also provide other forms of strength. For the black settlers referred to by Gilroy, combining elements from the West Indies or Africa (highly specified as to island or country) with aspects of St. Pauls or Moss Side, linking global and local, may produce a new specificity, and a new source of identity — Black *and* British. But you may remember — once again from TV10 — that Gilroy discussed some of the real problems in putting together such an identity.

The interests of different groups are served, in other words, by the dominance of particular representations of places. Different representations are often really competing claims about the nature of society. And representations of places can have effects. Edward Said, after his analysis of the construction of the image of the Orient for Western Europe, goes on to argue that that representation was in turn used as a means to dominate the Orient (Duncan and Duncan, 1988, p.123). The conflict over images of parts of the inner city has also had its own effects. Sir Kenneth Newman, Metropolitan Commissioner, gave yet another view of parts of the inner city. After enumerating some characteristics of certain areas of London with a high-percentage black population, he wrote: 'If allowed to continue, locations with these characteristics assume symbolic importance a negative symbolism of the inability of the police to maintain order. Their existence encourages law breaking elsewhere, affects public perceptions of police effectiveness, heightens the fear of crime and reinforces the phenomenon of urban decay' (Newman, 1983, cited in Gilroy, 1987, pp.108–9).

In other words, as Newman makes clear, the real danger associated with these areas arises not so much from 'mugging' or 'riots', but from their very symbolism as places.

———————————————— ACTIVITY 3 ————————————————

1   Who has the image of the north west which is pictured in the Lowry painting?
    • locals? which locals?
    • business people based in the south?
    • executives of multinationals, based abroad?
    • southerners in general?

2   If you think that at least some 'southerners' have this image, *why* do they have it?
    • to bolster their feelings of superiority?
    • to pin down in this relatively harmless caricature the slightly threatening 'great unknown' which lies to the north of the Watford Gap?

- because they are simply 'behind the times'?

IT'S TIME SOMEONE PAINTED A NEW PICTURE OF THE NORTH WEST

If this is how you visualise the North West, you're certainly behind the times. A confident new spirit of enterprise and commercial creativity has swept the region, leaving a new air of prosperity.

Now, in a unique collaboration, under the banner of 'Fast Forward - The North West Direction', Granada Television and seven of the area's principal economic development agencies are hosting a four-day series of televised business forums from the 1st-4th of November. Prominent business personalities and the heads of leading national and international companies are invited to attend and involve themselves in debates concerning the North West's enormous potential.

We'll be examining the numerous investment opportunities created by the region's economically buoyant state,...so if you're in a position to contribute and benefit from Fast Forward's in-depth analysis and discussion, simply contact:

LAUREN WILSON 061-832 7211 ext 3230

FAST FORWARD
THE NORTH WEST DIRECTION

1 - 4 NOVEMBER · GRANADA TELEVISION · STAGE ONE · MANCHESTER · ENGLAND

Figure 1   Advertisement for the north west

3   Why is it important to some of the groups which sponsored the advert to mobilize a *different* image of the north west?
   - what kind of an image do you think it will be?
   - will it be 'true'?

These questions don't have simply 'right' or 'wrong' answers. Try to use the arguments in this section to think about them. Maybe you can provoke a discussion with someone.

SUMMARY

- Different social groups may have different representations of a given place.
- Such social groups may be defined in many ways — for instance by class, ethnicity, gender, religious group, or by being insiders or outsiders to the place.
- A 'representation' of a place, in this sense, may include the overall image which a group has of the place, their idea of its past history, their mental maps of the area, and even contrasting meanings attached to individual buildings.
- The fact that this applies just as much to the past of a place as to its present means that we cannot identify 'real places' by looking into history. Authenticity is just as hard to find in history as it is in the present.
- These distinct representations held by different groups may compete and conflict with each other.
- Representations of places reflect and relate to structures of power and may be used both in the interests of domination by powerful groups and as sources and symbols of solidarity by those who resist.

2.2   LOCALITIES

If we go back again to our question, 'Do places have their own local character?', while we have just explored the meaning of 'local character' and its representation, there is another term which must be explored further — 'places'. What do we mean by 'a place'? It is amazing how we can use a term like this so often and yet be stumped, as most of us are, when it comes to giving a precise definition of it.

Let us clear some ground immediately. In the geographical literature, the term 'place' usually does not refer simply to some spatial extent of the earth's surface which has an administrative boundary-line drawn around it, although these are often used as shorthands — for example, Yorkshire, the Borough of Hackney. Such boundaries may be very important to people's lives. The politics of the local council may be quite different on one side of the boundary from that on the other (on one side the council may be levying high local taxes, there may be a meals-on-wheels service and an equal opportunities committee, while on the other side the council may be levying a low local tax but maybe providing none of these things). In the case of Yorkshire, if you're male and have been born within the boundaries you are eligible to play for the County Cricket Club, otherwise you will be deprived of that particular honour (although, even as I write, there are debates about whether this rule should continue!).

The existence of such boundaries does not in itself define places in the sense we are grappling with here. On the other hand, the effects such boundaries produce may indeed be part of what gives particular character to a place. But that provides us with a clue — when we use the term place here we are defining it in relation to *the geography of social processes*.

In the course up to now you have studied a wide range of social processes — sociological ones, economic, political and psychological — and each of these has its own geography. As we saw in the last section, the different social groups carved out their own 'places' within Hackney, the daily, weekly, yearly lives of each revolving around geographical foci and networks particular to themselves. The geography of those daily lives could be described as 'activity spaces', that is sets of routes and spaces tied together by the activities of these particular agents within society. In these cases the activity spaces are probably on the whole quite local, quite small scale, linking home, shops, friends, work and place of worship. But if we think of other social processes, then it is clear that their geography may be as wide as the world itself. The activity space of the financial sector spans the globe. The possibilities for investment, or the provision of financial services, in principle exist anywhere. The main centres of activity are in New York, Tokyo and London. There is constant traffic, in people, in information, in money, between them, and one does not go to sleep before the next has woken up, to maintain the chain of twenty-four-hour dealing.

The complexity and variation in such activity spaces is enormous. Multinational corporations span the world (though that does not mean they cover all of it for there are vast areas which they ignore as not offering investment opportunities). But the local bakery may have quite a restricted reach, in both its suppliers and its customers. The 'local' village may indeed seem to be isolated from such global movement. But is it? The bank (if there is one) will be part of a multinational financial institution, local residents may go abroad for their holidays or have friends and relations who have emigrated, the suppliers to the local bakery are in fact most likely to be amongst the biggest transnationals in the world (remember afternoon tea?), and where does the petrol in the garage come from? Even that classic symbol of the English village, the church, is of course part of a religion which has its roots in lands far from the UK. One way of standing back and viewing the society in which we live is indeed as a highly complex, interlocking set of such different activity spaces, each belonging to particular social processes, and defined by them, but with their geographies overlapping and interlocking with each other.

So when you go to the bank, you are tapping into an activity space which links your activity to things happening in Tokyo, or to Latin American people enduring austerity policies so that their governments can pay the debts they owe. In Unit 21 it was argued that the 'micro-reality', for example the routine of daily life, is what provides the 'glue' of the bigger structures of society. It is an important part of the mechanisms by which such structures are maintained, and changed. Here we can see that those different levels of society also have distinct geographies. Yet, again, each is essential to the other. The local activity spaces of our daily lives are thus linked into global spaces — and neither could exist without the other.

A number of theses have been put forward about these geographies and how they are changing. Let us examine four of them here. As you will see, they do not necessarily contradict one another, but they do stress different aspects of current changes.

1 One of the most evident features of life in the twentieth century (or at least in twentieth-century UK) is internationalization. The growth of multinational corporations, the increase in foreign travel, the apparently inexhaustible supply of goods (from exotic fruit to foreign films) from other countries — all are evidence of this phenomenon. You can now fly to New York from an airport in the UK in less time, as has often been remarked, than it took not so long ago to get by train from London to Glasgow, for instance. It is a phenomenon referred to as 'time-space compression' by David Harvey, one of the geographers who have argued this thesis most strongly (Harvey, 1989). What it implies is a kind of 'shrinking of distance'. A particular measured distance in kilometers can mean something very different depending on if you have to 'cross it' by foot, by 'plane' or by fax. *The first thesis is that in general distances are, in the current period, getting shorter.* The examples of internationalization given above bear

witness to this fact. But do you think it is universally true? Can you think of any examples where distances seem to have become longer? Where particular places are more inaccessible than they used to be? If you live in a rural area (or even in some parts of our major urban areas) and do not have the use of a private car you may well answer strongly in the affirmative!

2   But what that in itself makes clear is that it is not distances themselves which change (distances are of course in that sense *not* getting shorter) but our social relationship to them. For a small group of people in this country (mainly male, mainly white, mainly in certain highly internationalized sectors of the economy) having a conference call with Singapore or Los Angeles, or even going there physically for a meeting, is a relatively common occurrence, not one to be particularly remarked upon. For others, on low incomes perhaps and/or without a car, or with particular 'constraints' such as pre-school children and no local provision of nurseries, or senior citizens in areas where there are no bus-passes, the geographical horizons of life may seem to be closing in. (Yet even those who hardly ever go out may increasingly receive radio and television programmes, and perhaps buy commodities, produced around the world.) The point is that activity spaces are socially constructed and differentiated. *The second thesis, then, is that there is growing inequality in the spatial horizons of different groups within the UK.*

3   According to a third thesis, the biggest difference in the current ability to 'annihilate space by time' is between companies and their employees or, more generally, between capital and labour. This is really a particular case of the second thesis. On the one hand, it is argued, industry is becoming more mobile. It is less tied down by the need to be near natural resources, while improvements in both transport and communications have dramatically reduced the 'costs of distance' for many kinds of production. Not only do individual corporations have plants in many different countries, but they actively choose between them, and indeed play off one against the other when seeking to make a new investment. So the announcement that, for instance, a Japanese electronics or automobile manufacturer is thinking of building a new plant in Europe will immediately spark off a competition between a host of local areas right across the European Community, each staking their claim to be the most appropriate location (or to be the one which offers the most in the way of subsidy) for that particular piece of 'mobile investment'. For much capital investment is mobile in that sense these days. It will matter to it where it locates — the investment is unlikely to be completely indifferent to location, or 'footloose' — but the company could probably operate, and make a reasonable profit, at any one of a number of places. For the groups of local workers competing for the investment, on the other hand, represented through their councils, their unions, or through a local Industrial Development Agency (remember the advert for the north west of England in the last section), the choice of location by the company will make a huge difference, possibly between unemployment and a job, and certainly also to the economic structure and character of the areas in which they live. Multi-plant companies can also play off one plant in one location with another elsewhere, comparing wage-rates or levels of productivity and threatening to pull out of one if it does not come up (or down) to the levels of the other; or plants can simply shut-up-shop and move off elsewhere where conditions are now more propitious. While capital is thus becoming more mobile, labour although able on occasions to migrate (although international migration of labour is severely restricted by many governments) and certainly increasing in its degree of international organization and contact, still remains much more fundamentally rooted to the reproduction of daily life within much smaller areas. The activity spaces of labour and capital, broadly speaking, are changing in contrasting ways and expanding (where they are expanding) to very different extents.

One thing which it is important to notice about both theses 2 and 3 is how they relate to power. Industry's greater geographical mobility and its wider activity spaces strengthen its hand in the balance of power between it and labour. The greater span of the activity spaces of some groups in society as compared to others may reflect, and reinforce, the greater status and influence of those groups.

4   There is a further thesis, too, which would say that *both the international level and that of the local area are becoming more important.* Here the argument is two-fold. On the one hand, it is argued that internationalization is making the national level less important. Whether it be multinational corporations, international finance, or the European Community, the role of the nation-state is set to decline. (You have already studied some aspects of this in Unit 14.) On the other hand, it is argued that the regional level might be becoming less important than the local (in the sense of sub-regional), particularly as the big mining and manufacturing industries, which dominated whole parts of the country, have gone into decline. In the next section we shall be exploring the very similar case of Lancashire cotton. Once the basis of the economy of the whole region, that industry has now declined and a greater variety of activities have taken its place. You will also have a chance to take further some aspects of this debate in Unit 25 later in this block. Moreover, it is precisely this thesis, and its relation to the first one (the one concerning time-space compression) which is addressed in Chapter 19 of the Reader by Kevin Robins, and which you should read at the end of this section. Robins is arguing that there are currently major changes under way, not only in the way the economy is organized but also in the cultural sphere, which are altering the geography of our lives. Not only is there in some senses a re-emergence of 'local' themes but even more importantly, he argues, the global level is even more significant. These are, he argues, precisely 'global local times'.

We are here, therefore, taking our *local-global* theme of the course a step further. All these theses and the article by Robins are arguing, not only that there is a relation between local and global, but that the meaning of it and the nature of it can change over time. Note also, however, that in this thesis (and also in Unit 25) the term 'local' is used to mean smaller than regional.

But how are activity spaces related to 'places'? One argument that is now increasingly made by geographers, and about which there is considerable debate, is that 'places' are formed through the meeting of lots of different activity spaces at particular geographical points. So, for example, if we think back to the discussion of Hackney, we know that it is formed out of the activity spaces (each of them different) of a range of different groups of people. These are local activity spaces. We also know that it is linked into the activity spaces of building societies, which are probably national. There are probably banks with national and international links. We also know that Hackney is *excluded* from some activity spaces — some of the big supermarkets and chain-stores, for instance, have either left or never arrived. The people of Hackney, with their diverse backgrounds link it in other ways — cultural and familial — to a range of international activity spaces. The point we are making here is that part of what places are, and part of what gives them each their uniqueness, is this particular mix of interlocking activity spaces which is present in each.

We can now recapitulate our previous discussion and spell out this point in more detail. *First*, this argument says that places are constructed through social activities and must be defined in terms of them. *Second*, it also recognizes that the various activities that go to make up society each have their own internal geographies, which also change over time. For example, a locality within which the branch plant of a multinational company is located has a very different relation to the overall activity space of that company, than does the locality where the headquarters is sited. It has a different role within the spatial structure of the multinational, and that will have its own effects — in terms of the types of employment it brings for example. *Third*, however, in any particular geographical area such activity spaces overlap and, most important-ly, the social activities which construct them probably interact. *Fourth*, this overlapping and interaction can create new, place-specific effects. Thus, the various activity spaces within a locality may produce conflicting interests (locality emphatically does not mean community in the sense that all live together in conflict-free harmony), they may interact in a whole variety of ways or, perhaps more rarely, they may simply co-exist with the reality of each having no impact on the other. But simple co-existence or active interaction, it is part of what produces the particularity, or local character, of a place. This kind of conceptualization — to distinguish it from the old concept of place which alluded primarily simply to a particular geographical area — has been called a *'locality'*.

So, a locality is a 'place-based' concept in which are brought together many diverse activity spaces.

Let us then go to some 'localities', some broadly-defined regions of the United Kingdom and examine them in relation, in particular, to the *international* activity spaces in which they are embedded. And in that context we shall examine further the theme of the local and the global.

SUMMARY

- Social processes and activities have their own particular spaces of operation, which we can call their activity spaces.

- These activity spaces are different for different kinds of activity, and have their own internal geographies. The activity space of a multi-plant company, for instance, is centred on its headquarters, with branch plants on its periphery. The activity space of your daily life may be centred on home, but with other places playing major or minor roles.

- There are a number of theses about what is happening to the geography of social activity: (i) that there is time-space compression, (ii) that the activity spaces of different groups are unequal and getting more so, (iii) that one example of this is the difference between the activity spaces of capital and labour, and (iv) that it is the global level and the sub-regional (or local) level which are important today.

- A place (or 'locality') may be defined as the meeting point of a number of distinct activity spaces, and the interaction of these activities may in turn produce further effects, particular to that place.

===== READER =====

Now turn to Chapter 19 of the Reader, 'Global local times' by Kevin Robins (pp.196–205). As you read the chapter, it would be useful to have to hand a note of theses numbers 1 and 4.

3   REGIONS IN THE WORLD

3.1   LANCASHIRE AND COTTON

We have now established some basic principles about places and how geographers look at them. The aim is to use some of that understanding to explore the geography of the United Kingdom.

From the late eighteenth century until the 1930s the economy of the north west of England, especially of Lancashire, was built to a considerable extent on the cotton textile industry. In 1841 over one-third of all the workers of the north west region registered in the Census worked in textiles (Lee, 1979), the overwhelming majority of them in cotton.

It is a classic case, of the kind referred to in Section 2, where the dominant imagery of a part of the country was tied up with the dominant industry. So let us examine this imagery: the five and six storied mills with their towering chimneys, the name of the millowner written proudly lengthways down them, women workers at spinning machines, the clatter of clogs on setts at the change of shift. The utter confidence of the red, Victorian merchants' buildings in Manchester — those of us who come from there grew up with the idea that 'what Manchester thinks today London thinks tomorrow'. The poverty of the 1930s and the devastation of the cotton towns, the long slow decline of the industry. Until today when, although the industry still exists, it is in changed form and no longer dominates and there are Heritage Centres in Wigan, and Quarry Bank Mill in Styal (remember TV03?), to remind us what it was like in the days when Cotton was King.

And yet — it hardly needs saying but it is important to remember — no cotton grows in Lancashire. The industry, and all the ancillary activities with which it dominated the region for so long, depended throughout for its central raw material on an import. Moreover, it also depended on other countries for its markets, for most of the cotton cloth which was produced in the region was made for export. Even as early as the beginning of the nineteenth century, around two-thirds of its output was sold abroad.

This, then, was the dominant image. Moreover, as the Activity at the end of Section 2.1 showed, it is still one to which reference is made. Further, while it is an image based on the past, it already has many international links. So let us explore the case of Lancashire further, to analyse in a bit more depth this relation between local characteristics and more global phenomena. How does this relate to our theme of local and global?

The momentous changes which took place in Lancashire in the eighteenth and nineteenth centuries were local changes, but they were the start of something which was to spread far wider. For what happened in Lancashire over this period was not just the growth of the cotton industry but the birth of industrial capitalism. It was a change in the manner in which production took place. 'It was not Birmingham, a city which produced a great deal more in 1850 than in 1750, but essentially in the old way, which made contemporaries speak of an industrial revolution, but Manchester, a city which produced more in a more obviously revolutionary manner' (Hobsbawm, 1968, p.34). Both Unit 1 and Unit 10 and also Chapter 1 of the Reader, have examined the kinds of social transformation which this involved. Factory production with regular hours took over from production in the home. The labour process was completely reorganized, the division of labour was reinforced so that individual workers did more and more specialized tasks, and the beginning of mechanization meant that the pace of work was controlled by the movement of machines. New divisions emerged in society (for example, as Canon Parkinson wrote about Manchester):

> There is not a town in the world where the distance between the rich and the poor is so great or the barrier between them so difficult to be crossed ...

> There is far less *personal* communication between the master cotton spinner and his workmen, the calico printer and his blue-handed boys, between the master tailor and his apprentices, than there is between the Duke of Wellington and the humblest labourer on his estate.

> (quoted in Messinger, 1985, pp. 22-3)

The 'distance' which Canon Parkinson was talking about was social distance. But, as we might expect from the last section, those social divides were reflected geographically. As in Hackney two centuries later, there were different activity spaces for different social groups within one town:

> In Manchester the poor in their courts and cellars lived 'hidden from the view of the higher ranks by piles of stores, mills, warehouses, and manufacturing establishments, less known to their wealthy neighbours — who reside chiefly in the open spaces of Cheetham, Broughton, and Chorlton — than the inhabitants of New Zealand or Kamchatka...'
> ...'Ardwick knows less of Ancoats than it does about China'.

> (Thompson, 1968, pp.355–6)

So was there one place called Manchester? There were clearly different activity spaces for different social groups, in this case groups defined in class terms. 'The place called Manchester' contained the activity spaces of these very different groups, and these in turn were set in the global space of the cotton industry. This way of thinking about the place also immediately throws light on the theses in the last section which argued that the activity spaces of different groups in society are getting more unequal. While it is not possible to say from that last quotation whether the inequality is now worse, it is certainly possible to say that it is not new. While the poor (labour) lived lives tied to their local area, capital roamed the world bringing in raw cotton and selling it abroad.

On the one hand there was the growth of a working class, on the other the rise of a class of industrialists. One of the most successful of the early cotton millowners was Sir Robert Peel (1759–1830), who established a calico-printing firm in Blackburn. His son, also named Robert, well set on the road, joined with some ex-partners of his father in a firm in Bury. It prospered; new branches were set up in new locations and the company expanded its activities within the cotton industry, and the young Sir Robert became a baronet, a member of Parliament and later Prime Minister, an acknowledged representative of the new class of industrialists.

Sir Robert Peel (Junior) became Prime Minister of the United Kingdom, not Lancashire, and when we talk of the class he represented we talk, very often, in national terms. And the changes inherent in the early Industrial Revolution were in some senses 'national' changes. In fact, *like all social processes, they happened unevenly*. In this case, not only did the birth of industrial capitalism happen in one country before others but also it happened in one part of that country. The Census of 1841, quoted earlier, shows that nationally nearly a quarter of all those recorded as in employment worked on the land, in agriculture and in other activities. In all regions except the north west, the proportion was over 10 per cent. Nationally, the 'dominant pattern of employment distribution lay in the division between rural labour and various categories of service employment in the towns' (Marshall, 1987, p.145). So Lancashire was highly exceptional in the economic geography of the United Kingdom in the first half of the nineteenth century.

But if this is a clear example of a social process occurring unevenly over space, the *way* in which the local changes in Lancashire became more global is disputed. This is even true of its influence on the national economy. On the one hand, the international character of the cotton industry meant that it did not have many links to the rest of the UK economy. It did not stimulate much growth in other sectors. Since all its raw material was imported it did not stimulate any production of inputs'and since most of its output was exported there was little impact on industries which might have processed it further. In other words, it was argued that in this way, and in comparison with many other industries, cotton manufacture had fairly few economic effects on the national economy (Habakkuk and Deane, 1963). It is also argued that, while important regionally, cotton never represented a very high share of national output (Deane and Cole, 1967). But data from that early period of industrialization is notoriously difficult to work with.

Other research has challenged Deane and Cole's estimate of the importance of cotton output in the national economy and argued that it was significantly greater (Chapman, 1972). Chapman also challenges the argument that the impact of the cotton industry on the wider economy and society was low. He agrees that the immediate effects on other industries were small. But he argues that there were longer-term impacts. It was the cotton industry which was the first to introduce standardized machinery. The first passenger-and-freight railway line linked Manchester and Liverpool. If there were not major effects nationally, there were locally — the cotton industry was part of what stimulated ironfounding, engineering and chemicals industries in the textile areas. Shipbuilding was encouraged by the demand from overseas trade, and that in turn provided increased demand for iron and coal.

Finally, as other authors stress, the cotton industry probably contributed more to the accumulation of capital, and to a shift of income from labour to capital, than did other industries (Hobsbawm, 1968, p.69). This in turn resulted from the combination of the rapid mechanization of the industry and the payment of extremely low wages, especially to the thousands of women and children who were employed in the mills. To complete the circle, the capital amassed in the hands of owners was used to invest in other sectors, for instance railways, and thus helped spread the process of industrialization, while the low wages which were its necessary counterpart (and the fact that in the early years cotton was almost alone as a developed industrial sector) meant that within the UK there were insufficient people with enough income to provide a domestic mass market. So the dependence of cotton on foreign markets — and thus its vulnerability to changes outside the country — was reinforced.

Now, there are three reasons why this kind of debate is important to the argument of the course.

First, it gives you a flavour of some of the debates about regional and industrial growth — some of the mechanisms of uneven development — which you will be examining in more detail in the next unit.

Second, it is a good example of how, in debates between social scientists, there can often be points of agreement as well as disagreement, and also that there can be different *kinds* of disagreements.

—————————————— ACTIVITY 4 ——————————————

On what is everybody, in this debate about the impact of the cotton industry, agreed?

But in what different ways do they disagree? Find at least two contrasting examples. (You will be able to pick out the answers from the discussion which follows.)

———————————————————————————————

Third, however, this debate gives a flavour of something else. If what we have here is a good example of a social process occurring unevenly, and more particularly a local phenomenon (the birth of industrial capitalism) that was to become a global process, it was never certain that it would be so. Though most 'general processes' may have local origins, relatively few local social changes become more generalized. And at the time, at the turn of the century from eighteenth to nineteenth, it must have been difficult to tell. Just as Unit 14, discussing the global political changes of today, spoke of feeling at a moment of historical transition with the future uncertain, so it must have seemed then. The lack of direct links to the rest of the economy, at least in the short term, must have made Lancashire cotton seem an isolated, perhaps a one-off, development. (Note that this lack of immediate links is what everybody is agreed on — did you pick that out in the Activity?) Moreover, the 1830s and 1840s were a period of economic instability and social discontent. Chartists, Radicals, Luddites, early trade unionists challenged the new order. Not only working class but middle classes agitated for reform. In Manchester itself in 1819 there was 'the Peterloo massacre', as it came to be called locally, when a gathering of around 60,000 mainly working class people from all over Lancashire, come to hear the famous radical orator Henry Hunt, was broken up by the local yeomanry. Panic and rioting broke out, and some people were killed (the precise number is still disputed), and hundreds seriously injured.

> At the time of the great Chartist general strike of 1842 every adult person in, say, Blackburn could remember the time when the first spinning factory and power-loom had been introduced in the town, less than twenty-five years earlier. And if the 'labouring poor' hesitated to accept the system as permanent, even less were they likely — unless forced, often by extra-economic coercion — to adapt themselves to it, even in their struggles. They might seek to by-pass it, as the early socialists did by free communities of cooperative production. They might seek, in the short run, to evade it, as the early trade unions did by sending their unemployed members 'on tramp' to some other city, until they discovered that 'bad times' in the new economy were periodic and universal. They might seek to forget about it, dreaming of a return to peasant proprietorship.
>
> (Hobsbawm, 1968, p.123)

Moreover, uncertainty about the future must have been heightened by the length of time it took for the new forms of production to become more widespread. (Note again, that this relates to the Activity you have just done. Some of the debate arose because of contrasting views of how to evaluate the impact of cotton. While some stressed the low immediate impact others, agreeing with this, stressed the longer-term repercussions. That was one way in which the parties to the debate disagreed. Another one you might have picked out was over how to interpret the data-source.) One way and another, however, it was a long and uncertain process which turned this *locally*-based revolution in the social organization of production into a more widespread *global* one.

Yet from the start *the fortunes of the economy of Lancashire and the economy of the UK were inextricably linked*. For a period the international trading position of the country as a whole rested heavily on cotton. At its height, around 1830, more than half of the UK's total domestic exports, by value, consisted of cotton yarn and cotton goods, while at the same time imports of raw cotton made up a fifth of the country's total net imports. When cotton expanded the British economy expanded, and vice versa, and the trading patterns of Lancashire industry helped fix the position of the national economy within the wider international division of labour. In that sense the local was linked to the global because it was impossible to explain the UK's position in the world economy without taking into account what was happening in one region. *UK international pre-eminence was, for a while, built on the labour and enterprise of the people of Lancashire*.

But it is at least equally true to argue that it is impossible to understand what was going on in Lancashire in those years without setting it in its wider context. This is so in a number of senses. First, and in direct counterpoint to the argument we have just made, *the growth of the cotton industry in Lancashire could not have happened without the wider position of the British economy being what it was*. The cotton industry grew in part because of the UK's already-established position within the world economy. The stimulus for its early growth came in considerable measure from the accelerating patterns of colonial commerce in the eighteenth century. Its raw material was almost entirely colonial. The early industry established itself in the hinterlands of the great colonial and slave-trading ports of Bristol, Glasgow and, especially, Liverpool. In the very early days almost the entire export of cotton goods went to colonial markets, especially to Africa.

Throughout, it was dependent on the rapid expansion of markets overseas, a strategy which was greatly aided by the policies of national government — by the navy, sometimes by colonization in other parts of the world, or by policies on foreign trade.

Further, *what happened in Lancashire was dependent on changes in other countries, on other continents*. Until the 1790s, the bulk of its raw material came from slave-plantations in the West Indies and was thus dependent on the complex triangular trade with both the Caribbean and West Africa. By the end of the eighteenth century it was getting its cotton from the plantations of the southern states of the USA. In the 1860s the great Cotton Famine, which resulted in a devastating fall in production, was caused by disruption of supplies because of the American Civil War. There is a statue of Abraham Lincoln in Manchester, in commemoration of those times. It was the same with markets. Towards the end of the nineteenth century the industry was exporting about 90 per cent of its product. By the end of the century too, that market was overwhelmingly in the 'underdeveloped countries'. Such markets were easier to penetrate than those of countries more like the UK, which were anyway rapidly developing their own industries, and often doing so behind protective tarrif barriers. The industries of Latin America and Asia were less competitive and less protected. In the early years this was particularly true of Latin America, which became the largest single market for its exports. Later it was India and the Far East which grew in importance. British policy in India is often argued to have destroyed what had been a thriving local textile industry. In the middle of the nineteenth century, the UK made about half of all the commercially-produced cotton cloth in the world, and the bulk of that came from Lancashire.

Such a position was a dependent as well as a dominant one. As other countries began to produce more of their own output, and more competitively, the vulnerability of the Lancashire industry was clear. The real crisis began after the

First World War. To take one example, before that war India had produced only about 28 per cent of the local textile supply whereas after it it produced over 60 per cent. Gandhi's campaign to rebuild the cotton industry had its effects. Between 1912 and 1938 the amount of cotton cloth made in Britain fell by more than a half and exports fell by about 80 per cent. Lancashire's exports were back at the level they had been in 1851. And unemployment devastated households throughout the county. *There is no way of understanding that 'local' history without setting it in its global context*.

And of course in that sense it was not a 'local' phenomenon at all. The rise and decline of the Lancashire cotton industry was part and parcel of the establishment and change of global political and economic structures. It was not just Lancashire that was involved in this, but Latin America, the West Indies, the Southern States, India, China … All of them were part of the same structures, processes and division of labour. This was the global geography, the international spatial structure — *the activity space* — of the cotton industry.

Chinatown, Manchester

Yet if all these various parts of the world were affected by the same processes, they were affected differently. The activity space of the cotton industry had an internal geography, and each part of the world had a distinct position within the global structures. Thus, when the United Kingdom produced half the world's commercial cotton cloth that greatly reduced, in the immediate term, the possibilities for other places to engage in major production themselves. Only one country at a time can be the workshop of the world. Later, of course, industrialization was to become more evenly spread. It has been argued, further, that while at one end of these international interdependences Lancashire's industry boomed, at another end in the southern USA, and partly as a result, slavery was intensified and perpetuated (Hobsbawm, 1968, p.20). It is well established that — one way or another — in a third continent the highly-developed Indian textile industry was ruined. And when struggles for political and economic independence began to have their effect in countries which had been colonialized the reverberations flowed in the opposite direction. Even within Lancashire there were geographical variations within the regional system of production. Liverpool, with its vast and diversified port activities, had a very different employment structure from Manchester which was above all the commercial centre of the cotton industry, and different in turn from the spinning towns around its outskirts and the weaving towns farther to the north. In the late 1920s about one-fifth of Manchester's workers were employed directly in the textile industry, though many more were dependent upon it, while in some of the spinning towns the proportion reached nearly 90 per cent (Rodgers, 1986, p.43). *So a single global process of change could have highly differentiated local effects*. The development of the textile industry in India, with the recession of the thirties, led to a decline of exports for the UK national economy as a whole, a serious rise in unemployment in Manchester, but total devastation in some of the smaller towns of south east Lancashire.

3.2 LINKS BETWEEN THE LOCAL AND THE GLOBAL

The foregoing brief presentation of a part of the history of Lancashire over the period from the late eighteenth century to the 1930s allows us to develop further the discussion of the 'local' character of places which we began in Section 2.

First, it adds to the argument about the relationship between past and present. It reinforces the argument that we cannot simply identify 'real places' by looking into history. The past is no more authentic than the present. Different groups will have had contrasting images of that past when it was their present — the poor of Ardwick, for example, the wealthy merchants of Cheetham, the traders who came to the city from abroad. But also, the dominance of cotton over the Lancashire economy was an extremely brief episode in its history. If the 'real Lancashire' is built around cotton, then it began only a little more than two centuries ago. Before that it was a rural area, with Manchester a rather stately smallish town. And for nearly half a century now, cotton has been of dwindling importance in the economy of the county. Since then engineering, chemicals, a growing financial sector, and services more generally, have been far more important in the economy. Yet to say that we cannot identify a 'real place' simply in its past (let alone simply the economic past) does not deny the point which was made in Section 2: there still is some relation between the present character of places and their past histories. That brief period 'when cotton was king' still has its resonances and influences in the Lancashire of today. The great importance of the female labour force in cotton gave women in Lancashire more economic independence than anywhere else in the country. Their attempts to unionize — in the face of both employers and male workers — and the rise in Lancashire, in the midst of all this tradition, of the suffragettes is still important in a part of the country where women's assumptions about their own autonomy are still stronger than in many other areas. Or again, in the days of cotton Manchester was the commercial centre, a role which is today rapidly expanding once more though in a transformed economic context. Even the buildings have been reworked, and their presence has had an influence. The empty mills for a while provided cheap premises for other industries coming into the area. And the Victorian head offices of many a proud cotton empire, built to last and designed to impress, are today cleaned and refurbished and an important part of a revitalized city centre.

Second, moreover, whatever the relation between past and present, the international links are not new. Lancashire provides a good demonstration that the notion of 'a global sense of place' is not one which applies only to the late twentieth century. If we are going through a new period of accelerated 'time-space compression' today, internationalization in itself is a process which began in general some centuries ago. As long ago as the later years of the eighteenth century, Lancashire looked outwards to the sources of its raw materials and its markets almost as much as it looked to London.

But further, that history of the cotton industry illustrates *the complexity of the links between local and global*, and it is that which we are going to examine now. In the discussion of Lancashire, each time we looked at the subject from a slightly different angle a different aspect of the link emerged. In fact, each time a significant point in the argument was reached, I italicized the relevant phrase or sentence. Those statements are reprinted in the left-hand column of Figure 2.

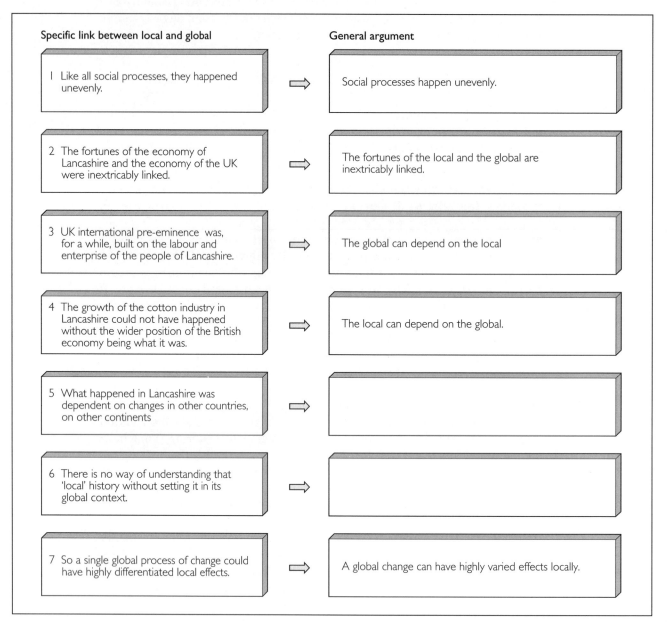

Figure 2

Specific link between local and global

1 Like all social processes, they happened unevenly.

2 The fortunes of the economy of Lancashire and the economy of the UK were inextricably linked.

3 UK international pre-eminence was, for a while, built on the labour and enterprise of the people of Lancashire.

4 The growth of the cotton industry in Lancashire could not have happened without the wider position of the British economy being what it was.

5 What happened in Lancashire was dependent on changes in other countries, on other continents

6 There is no way of understanding that 'local' history without setting it in its global context.

7 So a single global process of change could have highly differentiated local effects.

General argument

Social processes happen unevenly.

The fortunes of the local and the global are inextricably linked.

The global can depend on the local

The local can depend on the global.

A global change can have highly varied effects locally.

Our task now is to take what we have learned from this *case study* and organize it as a *general argument*. To do this, we have to translate statements about the relations between Lancashire, the United Kingdom, and the world, into arguments about 'the local and the global'. This we begin in column two of Figure 2, and I have done most of the translations. In some cases the statements were already in fairly general terms and so I have more or less just copied them across. Other statements I have generalized. Thus 'UK international pre-eminence was, for a while, built on the labour and enterprise of the people of Lancashire' I have translated as 'the global can depend on the local'.

There is an important point here, which is central to understanding the local-global theme in the course. You will see that in this exercise I have translated both 'UK/national' and 'international' as 'global'. This is because we are discussing the relation of both of them to Lancashire, which here is the 'local'. In its most general form, the local-global theme concerns the relation of local areas to wider areas. Thus in this example the UK is 'global' in relation to Lancashire. But as we have seen in Blocks III and IV, the UK can be local when we are considering it in the context of the world economy or international political structures. Likewise, if we were studying the local area Bolton, say, we would want to analyse it in relation to a set of wider (global) areas, possibly among them Lancashire. The term 'global' in our course theme does not always refer to the world level; the national level can be global from a regional point of view.

———————————————— ACTIVITY 5 ————————————————

Now complete Figure 2 by doing the remaining translations

Study Figure 2 for a while and make sure you know your way around it. If you are doing the TMA on your local area you could very well use the figure as a guide to some of your main lines of argument. You will certainly need statements 2, 4 and 5, for instance, and you may want to weave others in as well. It seems to me that there are three 'big statements' here:

1 social processes happen unevenly;

2 the fortunes of the local and the global are inextricably linked;

7 a global change can have highly varied effects locally.

The other statements are really elaborations of the second of these:

3 the global can depend on the local;

$\left.\begin{matrix} 4 \\ 5 \end{matrix}\right\}$ the local can depend on the global;

6 to understand the local you have to set it in its global context.

What these statements do is give us a framework, some important guidelines. What they do *not* do, however, is tell us how all these various influences are structured together, how they interact, which ones are more important and which less, and so on.

In fact the precise answer to these questions will depend on the particular issue we have in mind. Nonetheless, there have been some major general debates within the discipline of geography over the years about how these distinct 'scales' of explanation fit together. One such debate, which is still going on today, concerns precisely the kind of issue we have been addressing in this unit; that is: How do we set about explaining the character and fortunes of a particular region or local area within the UK? It is probably fair to say that in the early decades of this century the tendency would be to emphasize local factors in such an explanation. In particular, the physical characteristics of an area, its geology, scenery and climate, were often called upon in explanation of a region's particular economy and culture. Emphasis would be put upon the raw materials the people had at their disposal. At its most extreme, forms of environmental determinism would be used to explain the social and cultural characteristics of an area. Now it could be argued that eighty or ninety years ago the influence of the local environment, and of the availability of local resources, is likely to have been more important than it is today. This is true but we have also seen in this unit and in earlier units in the course (for instance as far back as Unit 1) that the regions of the UK have been linked into the international world for many centuries. So an *entirely* local explanation was perhaps even then inadequate.

In the 1960s almost a mirror-image kind of explanation grew up. This emphasized (and emphasizes, for it is still a very influential point of view) the international and national levels as being of overwhelming importance. In the sphere of economics (which is what it mostly focuses on) this theoretical approach sees the differences between regions as being essentially the result of global forces. In particular it would see 'the international capitalist economy' as being the crucial force at work. The writings of Harvey (1987, 1989) and Smith (1987) exemplify this approach. In their view the differences between regions are primarily the outcome of the way in which capital roams the world, using different regions in different ways. So the fortunes, and the character, of Lancashire over the period we have just been discussing would be explained primarily through the shifts over the same period in the organization of the international economy.

This theoretical approach remains important, and indeed there are probably few today who would dispute that in addressing the fortunes of regions within the UK these international economic forces are significant. Debate has, however, occurred over such things as *how* dominant such forces have been and how they should be linked with other kinds of causes. One important strand in this debate has been about the significance of local-level elements in the explanation. Thus, writers such as Urry (1981, 1987) and Cooke (1989) have argued strongly that any full explanation of the character of a region or local area must take account of both wider causes *and* local-level causes. Thus in the case of Lancashire, the particular characteristics of that county, its geographical characteristics and the nature of its society, were important in influencing the way in which it became linked into the international economy, through the cotton industry. Moreover, such a position would argue, any adequate account of regional differences must take in also cultural and political characteristics. This would include such things as voting patterns, the character of local authorities and their policies, and local social movements, for instance. It would also have to address the question: What is local culture (as we did earlier in this unit) and how can it be explained? As we have also seen, the explanation of these aspects of society can equally be argued to have international, national and local levels (see, for instance, Harloe *et al*, 1990).

These last two approaches remain in debate with each other today. What is interesting is how each successive approach of the ones described here grew up in part (but by no means entirely) as a kind of corrective to what it saw as the excesses of the previous approach. It should also be stressed, again, that there is no single formula for linking levels of explanation which will always work. It may well be, for instance, that in some parts of the country the international level has been a more important level of explanation than in others.

It is the international level which we are mainly exploring in this unit, but that is *not* because we think that level to be the only important one. The next unit will look more closely at causes of regional differences which lie at national and more local levels. Indeed, turning back to that last activity, it is the last group of more fully-elaborated statements that we are going to explore a bit further now. As you learned in Block III, in economic terms the United Kingdom is very open to the international world. So, while Lancashire was looking west to the Americas and east to India and China, while clerks in the merchant-houses of Manchester were certifying cargoes to Cuzco and Arequipa, and secretaries were sending off orders and invoices to Bombay and Shanghai, what was happening in other regions of the country?

Let us first examine two more cases in a little detail, and then we can go on to assess the wider picture.

3.3   SOUTH WALES AND CENTRAL SCOTLAND

In the middle decades of the nineteenth century, new regions were rising in economic importance to challenge the leadership of the north west within the national economy. They were the coalfields, most important among them south Wales, central Scotland and the north east of England. In 1850, the UK produced two-thirds of the world's coal, about half of its iron, and about five-sevenths of its steel. And most of it came from these regions. The regions also dominated the nation's shipbuilding — in 1870 about a fifth of all the ships built in the country were built on the Clyde, and even more on the Tyne. The balance of activities varied between the regions. There was a much wider range of industries in central Scotland and the north east of England than there was in south Wales, where the economy was massively dominated by coal and iron. But in all of them the regional economy was structured around this complex of heavy industries.

How then do our arguments about the local and the global apply in these cases? You will be examining the north east of England in TV12, so let us concentrate here on south Wales and central Scotland.

First of all, as in the case of Lancashire in earlier decades, there was a mutual interdependence between the economies of these regions and the national economy. On the one hand, had these regions been in another country they might not have developed at all in this way in these years. The pre-eminence which the UK economy had already achieved, through its mercantile traders and its cotton industrialists, provided the opportunity for and gave the spur to, the industries of these areas. It was on the back of this pre-eminence that the coal was exported, the iron was used to build the railways, and the ships for trade. The UK already had a head-start and demand for these goods was high. On the other hand, the UK could not have maintained such a dominant position in the world economy at this period without the major contribution of the people of these regions. I have already cited the figures for the *production* of coal, iron and steel. They were also very important *exports*, in the 1880s accounting for over a quarter of the UK's industrial exports.

But the *nature* of the links between local and global is very different here from in the case of Lancashire. Can you think in what way? In the case of Lancashire the raw material was imported, processed by local labour, and exported as manufactured goods. The pattern in the case of the coalfields of these regions was entirely different. There was no link abroad for the raw materials: in this period coal and iron were produced locally.

Much of the market for these goods was also found within the UK, and here too these industries differed from cotton. Yet even in this case there was a link to the international economy and to the country's place within it. While a considerable amount of coal was burned in the domestic fires of the rapidly-urbanizing population, much of it was used in the manufacture of other products. Iron and steel were used in building the railways, and the railways in turn increased the demand for coal. But these goods were also essential inputs into shipbuilding and shipping through which British trade became so dominant. Iron and steel are also essential in the manufacture of a host of other products from the export of which by the second half of the nineteenth century the British economy really was the workshop of the world.

But coal, iron and steel were also exported. From the middle of the nineteenth century about 40 per cent of the total national production of iron and steel was sold abroad. In general, however, the products of the coalfields were exported to different parts of the world from cotton. Coal, iron and steel were most in demand in countries which were themselves undergoing some degree of industrialization or at least in which a railway network was being built. The latter group of countries included many economies which were being opened up for the export of primary commodities. But the former group included also countries in Europe, and the USA. So while Lancashire looked primarily to the underdeveloped world for its markets, the great coalfields of south Wales and central Scotland shipped their products off to feed the building of railways in Europe, the North American prairies, Mexico, the pampas of the Argentine, and the Russian steppes; they were used to equip the goldmines of South Africa; and British steam-coal fuelled the world's ships. The Dowlais Iron Company in Wales, just to give one example, in the years between 1830 and 1850 supplied no fewer than sixteen foreign railway companies.

Nonetheless, by the later part of the nineteenth century the other industrializing countries ceased being so important as markets and became competitors. Coal and steel came to rely more heavily on the protection of the home market, in the case of coal including also the vast merchant fleet. Exports relied increasingly on the Empire and the underdeveloped world. By 1913 Argentina and India alone bought more British iron and steel exports than the whole of Europe, Australia more than twice as much as the USA (Hobsbawm, 1968, p.191). At this time, then, the pattern of trade became more like that of cotton, and indeed the cotton and iron and steel industries were important in establishing the UK's place in the world economy as an exporter of manufactured goods and an importer of raw materials (except for coal!) and food.

Like cotton too, the decline of these industries led to the collapse of whole regional economies. The decline of the UK's role as a major exporter of these goods, in other words a change in the place of the national economy in the world economy, led to the beginning of the end of industries which for decades had formed, and to some extent are still seen as forming, the 'local' character of major regions of the country.

──────────────── ACTIVITY 6 ────────────────

As a recap at this point, make a note of the ways in which the international links, of Lancashire on the one hand and south Wales and central Scotland on the other, differed from each other.

Of course, we have only examined a very small part of the history of these regions. There were and are many other activities and many other international links. In the early years of this century Manchester's Trafford Park industrial estate, the first of its kind in the world, attracted the first European investment of US companies such as Westinghouse and Ford. Indeed the estate was frequently characterized by its admirers as an island of 'American dynamism' within the UK economy. In recent decades, Lancashire has probably been better known around the world for some of its cultural products — for its football and the Beatles — than for its economy. And Manchester is being revolutionized again, with yet other links to the international economy taking over in importance. Its economy has been transformed, with a host of new activities growing up. Major concentrations of finance houses, a thriving Chinese community, a host of widely-acclaimed Chinese restaurants, and a new brand of music, are just a few of the things for which Manchester is now becoming known, and which are beginning to re-make its image.

There has been a revolution too in the relation of south Wales and central Scotland to the international economy. Although popular imagery of these regions is still tied up with coal and heavy industry (and male workers) in fact the new investment has been very different. One important sector of new investment (though still nowhere near as important to either region as coal and steel used to be) is electronics. In each area, though in contrasting ways, the electronics industry has transformed the links between the regional economy and the international economy. The activity space of the electronics industry is as international as was that of coal. But it is very different in its internal geography, and south Wales and central Scotland occupy different places within it.

Two faces of regional development: (above) a modern factory on the site of an old colliery and ironworks photographed from the Big Pit Mining Museum. (Below) the Big Pit Mining Museum photographed from the factory (above).

In south Wales in the entire electronics sector there is only one company of any size which (at the time that I am writing) is actually 'south Welsh'. All the others have headquarters outside the region, and in the case of the large amount of new investment which has taken place since the mid 1970s, almost all of these headquarters are also outside of the United Kingdom. An increasing number of them are in Japan. A first point to note about south Wales's new links to the international economy, then, is that it is subject to direct control through ownership from outside. Indeed this region has the highest degree of *external control* of its electronics industry of any region in the United Kingdom. Second, as many recent studies have shown (e.g. Morgan and Sayer, 1988), the south Welsh plants usually occupy a fairly lowly place in the international organization of these companies. They are at the 'low-tech' end of a 'high-tech' sector. Evidence for this is given by the fact that the Welsh industry employs a far lower proportion of professional engineers, scientists and technologists than the UK industry as a whole (though there are very recent signs that it may be catching up a little). Third, the current evidence is that a startlingly high number of these plants, and particularly the Japanese-owned ones, import their supplies of components (e.g. for assembling into television sets) from abroad, again often Japan. Fourth, the market for the goods produced is not only the UK but the European Community as a whole.

Such a structure obviously has many implications for the region, for the type of employment, and so forth, and much has been written about this. However, our object here is not to pass judgement on this, but to assess how the last two decades of electronics' investment in south Wales have moulded the region's links to the international economy.

Here, just in this analysis of one sector in one region we can see just how complex those links can be today.

They are equally complex, but different again, in the case of central Scotland. Here too the electronics industry has established a significant presence, and indeed the region is sometimes referred to as Silicon Glen! (See map on pp. 48–9.) The industry in this region has somewhat older roots than in south Wales, but once again the bulk of employment is in companies whose headquarters are outside the region. There is, in other words, a high level of external control. In 1983 Scottish-owned companies as a whole accounted for only 16 per cent of total employment in the sector. By contrast, another survey in 1985 showed that 48 per cent of employment was in plants which had their headquarters outside the UK. (So what percentage, roughly — granted the difference in dates of the data — was in plants which were owned by companies based in the rest of the UK — mainly England?) The first point, then, is that as in south Wales there is an important international ownership link. The direction of this link is, however, different. In central Scotland, US ownership is by far the most important, accounting for 42 per cent of all foreign ownership and for almost all the growth in employment between the late 1970s and the mid-1980s. Second, while most of the plants are dependent on the home country of the multinational (usually the US) for their advanced research and development the Scottish plants have both more of their own research going on and make 'higher-tech' products than do most of their south Welsh counterparts. The Scottish electronics complex, in other words, has a less lowly position within the international activity space of the industry than does that of south Wales. Third, however, while again a higher proportion of components is produced locally than in the case of south Wales, there is still a high degree of dependency on foreign-made inputs. In this case, however, the dependency is often on inputs from plants even further down the international hierarchy, especially those in the cheap-labour economies of south-east Asia. Thus, in the case of semiconductors, Henderson reported on his survey done in the mid-1980s:

... Scottish-produced wafers are assembled and tested in Southeast
Asia and then dispatched directly to the customers. National
Semiconductor assembles and tests its Scottish-produced wafers in its
Malaysian and Thai plants. General Instrument does the same in its
Taiwanese plant, and Hughes assembles under a sub-contract
arrangement in the Philippines and Hong Kong, but tests the final
product after return to its Scottish plant. So far, only Motorola has
developed a different arrangement. Though previously assembling its
semiconductors in Southeast Asia, Motorola now has a fully automated
assembly and test facility alongside its wafer fabrication plant [in
Scotland].

(Henderson, 1987, pp. 404-5)

Fourth, what of markets? As in the case of the industry in south Wales, these
are confined neither to the region nor to the UK, but extend throughout the
European Community. In many cases, the function of these plants is to supply
the whole of the EC.

SUMMARY

In Sections 3.1, 3.2 and 3.3 we have been focusing on the complex relation
of the local and the global, and assessing the economic history of some
regions of the UK in that context.

- The potential complexity of local-global relations is summarized in
  Figure 2 in Section 3.2.

- The activity spaces of the cotton, coal and electronics industries are
  all international. But their internal geographies are different. And
  Lancashire, south Wales and central Scotland at different times
  occupied contrasting places within them.

- Nonetheless what the regions share in common is that their
  economic histories for the last two centuries have been linked into
  the international economy. Their 'local' economies have been very
  definitely set in the global one.

---

4 FRAGMENTING UNITED KINGDOM?

It is clear that over the last two hundred years different regions of the United
Kingdom have risen and fallen in prosperity. Moreover, it is also clear that the
nature of growth and decline in a region can at least in part reflect the place of
that region in a wider set of international relations. But the fact that
individual places have risen and fallen in economic prominence means that the
patterns of regional growth and decline within the national economy as a whole
have also been transformed over time. So far in this unit we have focused
mainly on individual places. Now, in this final section, we shall step back and
look at the wider patterns which result from all these regional differences.
These differences between places — the economic variations and inequality
between regions in particular — are part of what we mean by *uneven development*. Given what we have just studied in Section 3, it is clear that the pattern
of uneven development in the United Kingdom has changed a number of times
in the last two hundred years.

In this final section, we shall retain the focus on the international level, but
this time we shall relate those global connections, not to individual places only,

but to the wider pattern of regional differences. There are two aspects to this. First, the argument is that since the Industrial Revolution the different regions of the United Kingdom have often had links with highly contrasting parts of the world. It is in that sense that the title of this section is 'Fragmenting United Kingdom?' Different regions, in other words, have *different* relations to the wider world. Second, we shall examine how the changing pattern of uneven development in the United Kingdom can itself be related to its changing position within the world economy. We are continuing, then, the exploration of the local-global theme, but this time in relation to geographical patterns of growth and decline — in other words, to uneven development.

We have already seen something of all this in the early decades of industrialization. Regions rose and fell in economic importance and economic prosperity in accordance with the degree to which they were pivotal to the wider economic development of the United Kingdom and to its position within the world. The early Industrial Revolution saw the rise of Lancashire (and also Shropshire and the Black Country). The later importance of steel, coal, railways and ships brought with it growth in south Wales, the north east of England and central Scotland. The period from the end of the nineteenth century until the inter-war years saw another pattern again. This was the age of imperialist expansion *par excellence*, and this time the lead regions were the west Midlands and Greater London, based on the new electric power and synthetic materials. From the Second World War until maybe the 1970s (there is debate about this) the lead industries in the economy were in fact more geared to domestic consumption, and the new industries were based on, for example, electrical engineering. Again it was the west Midlands and Greater London which benefitted. While new industries grew apace in these areas many regions in the north went into long-term decline, forming a basis of the north-south divide we know today. Finally today, as I write this, one of the major changes ahead for the future of the UK economy and its place in the world is the completion of the opening of the European internal market. Once again, as before, it will have effects on economic geography (on uneven development) within the country. All the indications are that this new adjustment of the place of the UK economy in the world (together with the impact of the Channel Tunnel) will, unless there is a firm and imaginative policy to counter it, further reinforce the growth of the south over that of the north. National changes happen unevenly, and produce uneven effects, between different parts of the country.

Yet throughout this two-century-long history there has been one constant, which I have not mentioned much yet. It is the dominance of London, the seat of government and location of 'the City'. From before the Industrial Revolution the City has been a crucial link between the UK economy and the rest of the world. In the days of the merchants, most of the merchants were based here. Not just the City but even many of the middle class in the south and east have long lived off earnings derived from the colonies and other places abroad. There has also been a draining of control from other regions towards the south east. Many of the companies which began outside the south east, and which grew to be major corporations, now have their headquarters in London. And in the current era, with financial and professional services being given pride of place within the economy, and employment within them becoming so important (and so well paid!), these sectors are an increasingly significant component of uneven development within the United Kingdom. It is also a component which reflects, once again, a relation between the UK economy and the world. London is now one of the three global financial centres. Remember the concept of activity spaces: the City of London is a key node in the activity space of the international financial sector. Links run round the world from here, through the global geographical networks of finance, banking and insurance.

Note the relation, once again, to the theme of the local and the global. Such links from, and to, the City are of vital importance to the functioning of the UK economy as a whole. They are part of what constructs its place in the world — truly here a global sense of place. They are a vital component, for instance, of the balance of payments figures. So the UK economy depends on the City. It is also often argued, however, that this dominance of the City actually works to the detriment of other parts of the economy, most particularly export-oriented manufacturing. Here we see how it is related to geography, to uneven development. For many of these other sectors (particularly manufacturing sectors) are based in other regions. Could the dominance of the City, and the part of the south-east economy which depends upon it, therefore be working *against* the economic prosperity of other parts of the country? Moreover, while it is from the south east and London that these particular links around the world stretch out, many other parts of the country have completely different links abroad. Their economies are set in very different — though still international — activity spaces. The examples of south Wales, central Scotland and the north east of England give one type of example. For them, as we have seen, some of the major links into the international economy run to other branches, and headquarters, of companies based in other countries. While the City functions as a centre of international financial control, could the future of some other regions be as offshore assembly-points for multinational corporations with their headquarters elsewhere? In that case it might well be argued that the regional economy of the UK was fragmenting.

It is often argued that

> The division between provincial industry and metropolitan commercial and financial interests remains one of the most enduring characteristics of British capitalism. It has played a major part in shaping both the internal contrasts between the British regions' experiences of economic development and in the external relationship between British capitalism and the world economy.
>
> (Marshall, 1987, p.140)

Whatever your answers to these questions, it is clear that processes at local, regional, national and international levels are intimately linked.

Moreover these issues are not just economic ones. The last section was mainly concerned with issues of economic development, but the first section of this unit dealt more with non-economic issues, such as the distinctive cultural characteristics of different parts of the country. How are these things related? I am not going to answer that question here (it is a huge issue), though we shall develop it through the block. But let me mention just one aspect. You may remember from Block I that the dominance of Lancashire was associated with the rise to power of a particular political philosophy — that of Free Trade. The Free Trade Hall still stands in central Manchester. Later, the industrialists of the west Midlands argued passionately that the maintenance of Free Trade — the lack of protection afforded to their production — was undermining their prosperity. What we see here is an example of fairly similar social groups, but based in different parts of the country, adopting contrasting political positions.

One question all this raises is; what about now? Is there a connection between regions and their economies, and their important social groups, and political and ideological positions? You will see a debate about precisely this, in relation to voting-patterns, in Unit 25. But if there can be such connections, which regions are dominant now? Clearly the City remains of central importance. But beyond that is it the culture of 'the M4 corridor', with its dominantly Conservative vote, its overwhelming emphasis on individual competitiveness, and the enterprise culture, which led the shift in economic ideology in the 1980s? This is the region where the lowest proportion of employees are members of trade unions, the region with the highest level of individual share-ownership, indeed the region where the highest proportion of people bought shares in the previously nationalized industries which were privatized in the 1980s. Is it this region which is most representative of the UK today?

But that raises other questions. For clearly not every part of the country shares the ideology and politics which is dominant in the outer south east. If that region is dominant, then what of the traditions of collectivism, solidarity and social conservativeness of the old mining areas, or the more cosmopolitan, ethnically-mixed, central areas of some of our larger cities, where public-sector trade-unionism (in health, education and local authority work, for instance) are important elements in the employment structure? Are they somehow now on the margins of British society? And what does that mean for notions of nationalism and the representation of British identity which have been explored in this course, from Unit 1, to Unit 17 in Block IV, and TV10 in Block V? And we shall pick up again in Unit 25 the issue of uneven development and politics.

Clearly, uneven development is a significant characteristic of UK society. To go back to the point with which this unit opened, there clearly still are very great differences between places even within the UK. For that reason alone, as social scientists, we must study it. But there is more to it than that. As I write, the north-south divide is high on the political agenda. There are labour shortages in the south while unemployed people in the north cannot afford — even should they want to — to move south to find work. National growth is being held back by regional inequality. This is just one small example. But the point is that *uneven development matters*. The next unit will pursue further the question of how, then, we are to explain it.

Ebbw Vale steel works (steel making ceased summer 1978)

SUMMARY

- For at least the last two centuries, the patterns of uneven development within the UK have been influenced by the relation of the national economy to the world economy.

- In economic terms too, different regions of the country have had, and continue to have, quite *contrasting* relations to the world economy.

- There are also related variations in politics and ideology — which raises again questions of national identity.

Map of Silicon Glen

REFERENCES

Chapman, S.D. (1972) *The Cotton Industry in the Industrial Revolution*, London, Macmillan.

Clifford, J. (1988) *The Predicament of Culture: Twentieth-century Ethnography, Literature and Art,* Cambridge, Mass, Harvard University Press.

Cooke, P. (ed.) (1989) *Localities: the Changing Face of Urban Britain*, London, Unwin Hyman.

Deane, P. and Cole, W.A. (1967) *British Economic Growth, 1688-1959*, London, Cambridge University Press.

Duncan, J. and Duncan, N. (1988) '(Re)reading the landscape', *Environment and Planning D: Society and Space*, vol.8, pp.117-26.

Gilroy, P. (1987) *There Ain't No Black in the Union Jack: the Cultural Politics of Race and Nation*, London, Hutchinson.

Gregory, D. and Ley, D. (1988) 'Culture's geographies: editorial', *Environment and Planning D: Society and Space*, vol.6, pp.115-16.

Habakkuk, H.J. and Deane, P. (1963) 'The take-off in Britain' in Rostow W.W. (ed.) *The Economics of Take-off into Sustained Growth: Proceedings of a Conference held by the International Economic Association*, London, Macmillan (pp.63-82).

Harloe, M., Pickvance, C. and Urry, J. (1990) *Place, Policy and Politics: Do Localities Matter?*, London, Unwin Hyman.

Harvey, D. (1987) 'Three myths in search of a reality in urban studies', *Environment and Planning D : Society and Space*, vol.5, pp.367-76.

Harvey, D. (1989) *The Condition of Postmodernity*, Oxford, Blackwell.

Henderson, J. (1987) 'Semiconductors, Scotland and the international division of labour', *Urban Studies*, vol.24, pp.389-408.

Hobsbawm, E.J. (1968) *Industry and Empire, The Pelican Economic History of Britain*, vol.3, Harmondsworth, Penguin Books.

Jackson, P. (1988) 'Street life: the politics of Carnival', *Environment and Planning D: Society and Space*, vol.6, pp.213-27.

Lee, C.H. (1979) *British Regional Employment Statistics, 1841-1971*, London, Cambridge University Press.

Marshall, M. (1987) *Long Waves of Regional Development*, Basingstoke, Macmillan.

Messinger, G. S. (1985) *Manchester in the Victorian Age : the Half-known City*, Manchester, Manchester University Press.

Morgan, K. and Sayer, A. (1988) *Microcircuits of Capital*, Cambridge, Polity Press.

Newman, K. (1983) *Policing London: Post Scarman*, Sir George Bean Memorial Lecture 1983, 30.10.83.

Rodgers, B. (1986) 'Manchester: metropolitan planning by collaboration and consent; or civic hope frustrated' in G. Gordon (ed.) *Regional Cities in the UK 1890-1980*, London, Harper and Row, pp.41-58.

Said, E. (1979) *Orientalism*, New York, Vintage Books.

Smith, N. (1987) 'Dangers of the empirical turn: some comments on the CURS initiative', *Antipode*, vol.19, pp.59-68.

Stedman Jones, G. (1971) *Outcast London: a Study in the Relationship Between Classes in Victorian Society*, Oxford, Clarendon Press.

Thompson, E. P. (1968) *The Making of the English Working Class*, Harmondsworth, Penguin Books.

Urry, J. (1981) 'Localities, regions and social class', *International Journal of Urban and Regional Research*, vol.5, pp.455-74.

Urry, J. (1987) 'Survey: society, space and locality', *Environment and Planning D : Society and Space*, vol.5, pp.435-44.

Wright, P. (1985) *On Living in an Old Country: the National Past in Contemporary Britain*, London, Verso.

ACKNOWLEDGEMENTS

Grateful acknowledgement is made to the following sources for permission to reproduce material in this unit:

Text

Wright, P. (1985), *On living in an Old Country: the National Past in Contemporary Britain*, Verso.

Figures

p23: Courtesy of Stowe Bowden Wilson; L.S.Lowry, *An Accident*, reproduced by kind permission of Manchester City Art Gallery.

Illustrations

pp 48/49: 'Map of Silicon Glen', Scottish Enterprise.

Photos

p14: Judy Harrison/Format; *p15*: Copyright David Williams; *p17*: Sefton Photo Library; *p19*: Maggie Murray/Format; *p34*: Sefton Photo Library; *p41*: Copyright David Williams; *p46*: West Air Photography.

UNIT 24 UNEVEN DEVELOPMENT AND REGIONAL INEQUALITY

TMA.

Prepared for the Course Team by John Allen

CONTENTS

T MA

1 INTRODUCTION

Much of the previous unit was concerned with showing how uneven development in the UK is connected both to changes in the international economy and to changes in the UK's role within that shifting international economic order. It was evident that the full picture of how regional fortunes have changed over time could only be grasped if these changes were set in the context of wider national and international relationships. Indeed, a process of geographical fragmentation could be seen to be at work, with different parts of the UK locked into very different relationships with the national and international economy. From all this it was possible to discern that much of what happens to the economies of cities such as Manchester or Liverpool, and to places such as 'Silicon Glen' in Scotland, may have little to do with what happens to the UK as a whole.

There is certainly truth in this, but it is only part of the story. Questions concerning the UK's changing internal economic geography — concerning the relationships between regions, and inequality within and between regions — are not satisfactorily answered by global explanations. So, in this unit we look inwards, as it were, to geographical divisions within the country and take up the question that was left unanswered at the end of the last unit, namely, 'How do we explain uneven development within the UK?'

By the end of this unit, I hope that you will be in a position to answer this question. As you work your way through the unit, you will see that each section takes you a step further towards a possible answer. In a moment, in Section 2, you will be introduced to three questions which open up the issue of uneven development along different lines of enquiry. These questions set up the framework through which key aspects of uneven regional development are explored in the rest of the unit.

Section 3 takes up a specific aspect of uneven development: the issue of natural resources and the idea that differences in the 'natural wealth' of regions play a part in any explanation of uneven regional development. Are some regions, or parts of regions, wealthier or more developed than others simply because of their natural resources? Can the growth of Aberdeen, for example, be attributed simply to the presence of oil and gas deposits beneath the North Sea? Or are such questions increasingly irrelevant in an age in which information and service flows are prized more highly than material resource flows? These are the kinds of issues taken up in Section 3 and they should be read as part of the build-up to the theoretical accounts of uneven development presented in Section 4.

In Section 4, you will find three explanations of uneven geographical development, one based upon neoclassical economics, another drawn from a school of thought known as the cumulative causation school, and a third whose assumptions are drawn from marxism. Each of these three explanations presents a different kind of 'theoretical mapping'. By which I mean that each theoretical explanation works like a map, guiding our way around the uneven economic geography of the UK. Above all, the theoretical maps tell us something about how and why the geography of the UK takes its present uneven pattern, and in what direction it is likely to change. Section 5 then pulls some of this thinking together.

In the final section, Section 6, we pick up one of the threads of the block and, for the second time, ask the question, 'Why does uneven development matter?' On this occasion, however, the question is concerned with the impact of regional inequality on the development of the national economy: how regional inequality affects patterns of growth in the UK and how it shapes the overall direction of economic change. Before we engage with these issues, however, there are the three essential questions to be asked about uneven development. And this, conveniently, takes us to the start of the unit proper.

2   A QUESTION (OR THREE) OF UNEVEN DEVELOPMENT

The first question to be asked about uneven development concerns the issue of geographical divides and how we experience them. In recent times, we have heard a lot about the 'Two Britains', the two parts of a nation divided into North and South. A line running across the country, usually from the mouth of the River Severn to The Wash, is said to divide the prosperous South from the ailing North. In fact, the idea of a boundary line is potentially misleading. Rather than a line it is a deep economic gulf that is said to separate the North from the South; a gulf which can be shown by a host of economic indicators, such as unemployment rates, average earnings, growth rates, and the quality of job opportunities. Moreover, this divide is not particularly new. A North–South divide was a prominent feature of the UK economy during the 1930s

Figure 1   The North–South divide (with standard regions shown)

depression, and in one form or another it reaches back into the nineteenth century. So what is the question?

Question 1: If the North–South divide is so distinct, why are 'local' divides within regions often felt more sharply?

If, for example, you live in Cardiff or in Newport in south Wales, two areas which have experienced growth of late, you may be surprised to learn that you are usually regarded as belonging to the 'less prosperous' North. A glance over your shoulder, however, at the pit closures that have eroded a traditional coal mining community, may serve as a reminder of your area's losses. Conversely, some people looking over to south Wales from the tin mining areas of Cornwall in the South West region may also be rather surprised to learn of their 'dynamic' Southern tag. And so too perhaps would much of the population of the declining Medway Towns in the outer South East. In fact, it may be the case that places such as Chatham have more in common today with battered towns in the North than with many other places in the 'dynamic' South East.

The same observation may well hold for the unemployed populations of inner cities on both sides of the North–South divide. Many people in Merseyside, for example, have life chances similar to those of people in some of the inner London boroughs; and, in a social sense, there is less 'distance' between these two groups than there is between many Liverpudlians and the inhabitants of prosperous villages in Cheshire on the other side of the Mersey. Closer to the North–South boundary, those people who have long experienced hard times in Smethwick or Wolverhampton, or prosperous times in Solihull in the West Midlands, must surely be confused by their regions' fluctuating economic fortunes which have taken them out of the 'prosperous' South into the North, and then back again, in less than two decades.

Rapid transformations, then, as well as local and regional uneveness, are the very stuff of uneven development. And this is the point: there is both hardship and affluence on both sides of the North–South divide. Within the North and within the South some areas have experienced growth, whilst others have slumped; some rapidly and others at a more gradual pace. Above all, the patterns of growth and prosperity do not mirror formal or administrative geographical boundaries; invariably they stretch across regions, by-passing some areas altogether. The 'sunbelt', for example — that broad strip of high-technology activity that runs across southern England — takes in parts of the South West, the South East and East Anglia. But not all areas within the 'sunbelt' are noted for their high-technology developments. Many of the older industrial towns in the southern stretch, Basildon and Bedford for example, have been virtually by-passed by the 'sunrise' industries.

So what kind of answer can we give to the first question of uneven development? To say that the pattern of uneven development in the UK is far more complex than a simple North–South divide is true, although not particularly revealing. We know that the idea of a North–South divide has a particularly strong imaginative hold as a representation of regional inequality. But this in itself requires explanation — we know as much from the last unit. Another tack, therefore, would be to say that uneven development is about more than mere descriptions of patterns of difference and division; it is also about explanations of uneven processes of development. Behind the differences in economic development within nations, within regions and between cities are a set of processes which work themselves out unevenly, some operating across the nation, cutting through regions, and others operating at a global level. More importantly, some processes can be seen to highlight broad divisions such as the North–South split, whereas others accentuate, say, a city–country divide.

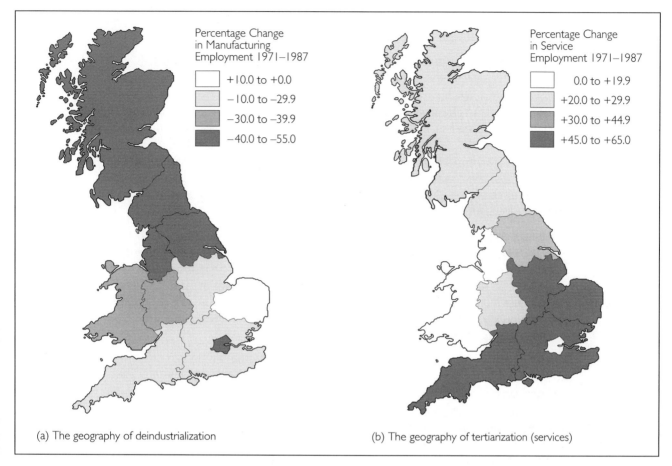

(a) The geography of deindustrialization

(b) The geography of tertiarization (services)

Figure 2   Changes in manufacturing and service employment, 1971–1987
Source: Department of Employment; Martin, 1988, p.223

For example, the North–South divide can be seen clearly in the shift in employment that has taken place in the UK in recent decades from manufacturing to service industries. As Figure 2 shows, since the early 1970s, job losses in manufacturing have been concentrated in the North, first in the old industrial cities and then in what had until recently been manufacturing growth regions, the North West and the West Midlands. Over the same period, service jobs have grown rapidly in the South, with the bulk ending up in the South East (although, interestingly, London has not benefited to the same extent). This pattern of employment makes it hard to avoid the conclusion that the old industrial heartlands of the North have gained the least jobs from the expansion of the service sector. What lies behind this clear pattern, however, is not one but a *set* of interrelated processes which have mapped themselves out unevenly.

Among the more important of these processes are, first, what has come to be known as 'de-industrialization'. This refers to an absolute decline in manufacturing employment in the UK. The global nature of this process and its local effects — namely, the manufacturing job losses sustained in the major industrial cities and the northern regions in recent decades — were discussed in Section 3 of Unit 23. The second important process is that of 'tertiarization' or, more simply, service sector growth. This process also has its origins in part in global economic changes, especially the internationalization of financial and commercial services. Banking and insurance, together with the commercial services that support them, are among the fastest growing sectors of the UK economy. And although they are concentrated in the City of London, these sectors exert considerable economic influence on the labour markets of the South East and (arguably) adjoining regions.

The third important process is related to the second; this is the shift from the public to the private sector of service job growth — a shift that started in the late 1970s and accelerated in the 1980s. There are two distinct geographies behind this shift. The first in that of public sector jobs which are fairly evenly distributed across the country, thereby lessening the unequal and uneven distribution of jobs; and the second is that of private sector services which are heavily skewed towards the southern half of the country. As a result of this shift, parts of the North are now increasingly dependent upon a public service job base, with places like Northern Ireland, for example, having just under half their total workforce in the public sector.

If we now put the geographies of the three processes together, superimposing each on top of the other as it were, then a pattern of the North–South divide is revealed. But — and this is an important 'but' — it is not the same divide as in the 1930s. It may look remarkably similar, and the boundary line itself may even follow a similar route across the country, but this new line is the outcome of contemporary economic processes rather than those which shaped the inter-war geography of the UK.

If we turn our attention from the North–South divide to the city–country divide, then there are additional processes that we have to consider. The city–country divide which arose in the 1960s took the form of an economic and spatial division between the decline of the inner cities and the growth of previously less industrialized, less urban areas and peripheral regions. If, as noted above, much of the collapse of manufacturing in the major industrial cities can be traced to the effects of de-industrialization, another process speeding that collapse was the decentralization of manufacturing jobs outwards from the cities. Some of those jobs crossed only short distances — to the outer suburbs of the cities or to the outlying reaches of a region; from London to the outer South East, for example. Other jobs, including some from service industries, moved further afield to the peripheral regions of the North and West of England. Decentralization, as a process, often involved the head offices of large UK and foreign-owned firms taking a decision to break up the large work places in the crowded cities and to set up branch plants or back offices in outlying, cheaper-cost locations. One of the advantages that such locations held for industry at that time was the availability of so-called 'green' labour — green in the sense that the workers, usually women, lacked experience of industry or of trade union organisation and its roots in a radical cultural tradition. In many ways, such work forces were the mirror image of the kinds of organized labour, predominantly male, that were left behind in the industrial cities in the 1960s and 1970s. Other advantages of decentralization included cheaper land and premises and, in some cases, closer proximity to markets. It was the pursuit of cheap 'green' labour, however, that illustrates something of the importance attached to this city–country divide.

Again, then, it would appear that certain economic processes give shape to some geographical divides and not others. Where you draw the line or lines of division, therefore, will to a large extent reflect the processes that you are interested in. Does this observation help us to answer the first question asked about uneven development — namely, why some of the divisions within and between regions appear more fundamental than the differences between the North and South of the country? I think that it does in part. It tells us that the lines between rich and poor regions, between depressed inner cities and bouyant rural towns, and also between North and South, are actually constructed through a variety of different social forces — political and cultural as well as economic. The main point, therefore, is that different processes, national and international, will shape the pattern of development across the country, at times reinforcing established divisions such as that between North and South, and at other times constructing new contours of felt inequality. And this insight leads into a second, broad question to be asked about uneven development.

Question 2: Does the success of some cities and regions depend upon the failure of others? Are the fortunes of places linked to one another?

We know from the previous unit that what happens in one part of the globe can shape what happens elsewhere. Think back to the example of Lancashire in the last unit and how its economic fortunes changed as a result of changes in the international division of labour. The development of indigenous textile industries in India and the Far East in the inter-war period was directly related to the demise of the cotton industry in places such as Lancashire. Development in one country led to underdevelopment elsewhere in the globe. Now if this kind of interdependency can hold at the international level, between countries, does it also hold within countries, between regions or between cities and regions? If places like the South East, or boom areas like the 'sunbelt', are 'winners', must there also be 'losers'? Would the same kind of logic apply to an oil-rich Aberdeen or to the expanding Docklands in the East End of London? If so, who are the losers? These are tricky questions. They are tricky because they imply something called a 'zero-sum game'.

A zero-sum game of development is one in which it is not possible for, say, the cities and the peripheral regions both to develop at the same time. If one develops, the other slumps. If, for example, the regions receive the likes of a Nissan or Toyota car plant then the cities with existing car plants may well lose out. In this kind of development game, increases in the competitiveness of an industry in one area are matched by decreases in the competitiveness of the same industry in another area, with a predictable result — a loss of jobs. In short, not all places can be 'winners'.

But just how plausible is this kind of development sketch? If a zero-sum outcome holds within one industry, does it also hold within one country? How true, for instance, is the assertion that the South of the country has developed at the expense of the North? Here it could be argued that the South East has attracted the leading-edge industries and more than its share of better paid, highly skilled jobs — both of which may have been placed elsewhere if a southern boom had not occurred. Alternatively it might be argued that growth in the South is the very basis of national growth. In this view, a booming South would bring benefits to the North as the pattern of growth fans out. Both views, however, stress intra-national connections, which we may wish to qualify. For example, we have seen that parts of the developing North, notably 'Silicon Glen', the location of Scotland's electronics industry, are locked into a set of US and Japanese interdependencies rather than any national interrelationships. Furthermore, we should not rule out the possibility of places in the North developing on the basis of their own natural resource endowment — oil and coal for example — which appear to owe little or nothing to developments in the South. All in all, these considerations revolve around the issue of whether urban and regional growth in the UK is independent *or* interdependent. This is one of the key issues that you should bear in mind as you work your way through the rest of the unit.

Finally, the third question to be asked about uneven development concerns the nature of development itself. So far, the notion of regional development has not been examined. The meaning of the term 'development' has been taken largely for granted, as if it were something transparently obvious. So the final broad question is:

Question 3: What is meant by the term 'regional development'? And who benefits from such development?

If, like me, you have (secretly) felt uncertain about the actual meaning of the term 'development', then the distinction between development *of* a region and development *in* a region is a useful starting point. Development *of* a region, as I understand it, involves the broad improvement of a region's employment structure, not just in terms of the number of jobs created but also in terms of pay, conditions of work and security of employment. There is also the question of the type of work that new industries bring to a region. Here, development *of* the region may imply an increase in the number of people who have marketable skills, or, relatedly, in the number who exercise a degree of control over their work — categories that could include multi-skilled manual workers as much as they do research scientists. In general, 'development of a region' suggests that most people in the region will reap some kind of benefit. This benefit may arrive either directly, through enhanced job opportunities, or indirectly through the economic spin-offs that new investment in an area can bring: the appropriately named 'multiplier effects'. For example, the entry of new firms may increase the demand for regional goods and services, that is, through the improved spending power of an enlarged workforce and through the supply needs of the firms themselves. Overall, then, the development *of* a region brings greater prosperity to the people of that region and raises their life chances.

Development *in* a region is harder to pin down. In many ways it is the opposite of the above, with development bringing fewer improvements to a region's workforce. Developments that do occur are likely to benefit the balance sheets of companies rather than a region's population. There is a sense here of regions being 'used' by industry. Typical of such development *in* a region would be the introduction to an area of industries that bring few jobs with them. This is the phenomenon known as 'jobless growth', which combines expanded profits with falling employment levels in an area. Think of the nuclear power industry or the chemical industry, for example, with their heavy capital outlay, or of some of the high technology developments in the electronics industry. None of these industries is known for its ability to generate plentiful jobs after the initial construction work. (Incidentally, the nuclear industry or, for that matter, any industry connected with toxic wastes raises another dimension to the notion of development *in* a region: in terms of environmental risks and general benefits, such industries are not likely to be regarded as particularly desirable).

Another example of development *in* a region is the establishment of the so-called 'screwdriver' plant. The term '"screwdriver" plant' refers to assembly-only plants of the sort established by, for example, many car manufacturers. Often set up by multinational companies to increase exports, this type of plant brings little or no technological know-how to a region. Research and development is carried out elsewhere, more often than not in the country of the parent company, and the extent of local commitment amounts to concern over how components are put together, and how efficiently they are assembled. Above all, the 'screwdriver' plant requires only unskilled or semi-skilled labour to assemble the product from imported kits. As a result, developments of this kind are said to use and reinforce the 'negative' characteristics of a region — particularly its cheap, low-skilled labour force. Few positive benefits are seen to accrue to the region, and little or no improvement to the life chances of a region's population takes place.

Chapelcross Nuclear Power Station, Dumfriesshire — development *of* or *in* a region?

As with many kinds of opposition, the distinction between development *of* a region and development *in* a region is drawn sharply in order to make a point. In this kind of abstraction, some of the detail has been thrown away so that the key features of regional development can be identified. True, much regional development is more complex than this, with some people and some places within a region benefiting more, and some less, than others. But if we start with the broad picture of development rather than with detailed descriptions we are often (although not always) in a position to identify some of the key processes involved. More importantly, the value of the distinction between development *in* and development *of* a region is that it questions the idea that *any* new development in a region is 'a good thing'.

This brings to an end our discussion of the questions asked about uneven development. That does not mean however, that the preliminaries are out of the way and that we can now move on to the task of explaining uneven development. In a number of ways we have been dealing with more than preliminaries — we have been dealing with ways of thinking about uneven development. And how you conceptualize uneven development is integral to your understanding of how it is produced and also reproduced. One way that you can hold on to this point is by completing the following activity. It acts both as a summary to this section and as an activity that takes the thinking of the unit a step further towards explaining the uneven and unequal development of regional economies.

─────────────────────── ACTIVITY 1 ───────────────────────

For this activity, I would like you to turn to the article in the Reader entitled *Economic and Social Change in Swindon*. Before doing so, however, read carefully the three questions set out below. Each question, as you will recognize, takes its cue from one of the three main questions discussed in this section.

(a) In the Reader article, the authors refer to a number of international processes that have shaped the changing economic fortunes of Swindon. Identify *two* aspects of international activity that lie behind the recent growth in Swindon's local economy.

(b) Is there any evidence — in terms of labour or other resources — to show that the relative economic success of Swindon has been at the expense of development in other parts of the UK? You will find that it is difficult to answer this question with any degree of certainty, so try to pull out a few possible leads.

(c) Finally, has the pattern of recent growth led to the development *of* Swindon or to development *in* Swindon? It will be clear that development has brought certain benefits to the area, but which social groups have gained and which have been by-passed?

READER

Now read the relevant Reader article, and, as you work your way through the piece, jot down any thoughts that will help you to answer the above questions. You may find it helpful to think back to the three questions asked about uneven development in this section, and to use these as a framework for reading the article.

Well, what answers did you pull out of the text? You may have found it easier to arrive at answers for questions (a) and (c), than for (b). I certainly did. Some of the possible leads I pulled out for question (b) are rather tentative. But let's take each in turn, starting with question (a). The first aspect of international activity that I identified was the role of inward foreign investment in Swindon as multinational manufacturing firms, mainly US owned, entered the local economy. This aspect comes across clearly in the text. Another aspect, though one that is less easy to discern, is the role of international finance. As Swindon's economy has become increasingly integrated into the regional economy of the South East, the town itself has benefited from the expansion of international services that has brought growth to London and the South East. Much of Unit 23 was concerned precisely with showing how such global connections come about and why they make a difference to the prospects of towns and regions. That is as far as I got. Did you notice any other aspects of international activity?

For question (b), I noted two possible leads. The first concerns the migration of skilled labour to Swindon, which may represent a direct loss from other regions. Certainly there is some national evidence to show that the poorer regions lose skilled labour to the growth regions (as you will see in Section 4.2), thereby reinforcing a cycle of decline. (The next Reader article, *Coming to terms with the future in Teeside*, makes a similar point.) The other possible lead that I identified is more circuitous. It concerns the use of public funds to finance infrastructure development — motorways and high-speed rail links for example — in the western corridor. Growth in this case consolidates growth and, arguably, attracts the sort of state money that leads to further growth — the big infrastructure development projects.

Turning to question (c), it is evident that growth has brought about an expansion of jobs in Swindon, many of a high-skill, high-status character, although equally many of a low-pay, routine, service nature. Economic growth, it would appear, has led to a greater fragmentation of the locality with some groups, particularly the skilled in-migrants, reaping considerable social and economic benefits whilst much of the working class could be said to have experienced development *in* rather than *of* the region. What do you think?

At this point, if you have been compiling a resource file on your town, city, or region, you may wish to make brief notes on the kind of answers that you would give to such questions were they addressed to your locality. You may also like to consider another aspect of regional development that has yet to be explored in this unit: the role that natural resources play in the development process. Swindon's initial development as a rail engineering works owed much to its physical landscape and accessibility to coal and water. To what extent has development in your region been attributable to an endowment of natural resources?

3 REGIONAL RESOURCES AND REGIONAL DEVELOPMENT

When you think of coal mining regions you probably call to mind south Wales, central Scotland, the North East, and perhaps also south Yorkshire and parts of the East Midlands. There are coalfields in other parts of the UK, yet few have become associated with the fixed imagery of the pithead in the way these places have. The previous unit spoke of this kind of regional imagery; that is, of images or symbols which capture a way of life, a set of routine cultural practices. There are many examples of this kind of association between areas and their industries that depend on natural resources: tin mining and western Cornwall has already been noted. Other familiar examples may be the association between red clay and the 'Potteries', or of ceramic tableware, especially Wedgwood, with the 'Potbanks' of north Staffordshire. All are disappearing associations, however, as these regions' economic heydays are long past. Nevertheless, other links between natural resources and regional industries do still exist.

Today, for example, there are connections between agriculture and the fertile soils of East Anglia, between oil and the Grampian region, especially Aberdeen, and there are the ties that remain between coal and 'its' regions. You can probably think of other less distinctive connections, for example, between salmon farming and the west of Scotland. Whatever examples you have in mind, consider the following question. Does an area develop simply because it possesses a natural resource base? Or, more accurately, does it develop because it has some kind of 'natural' advantage over other regions? Take coal in south Wales as an example. Did the presence of coal lead inevitably to the development of a coal mining industry in the region? And, similarly, did the presence of oil and gas deposits off the north east coast of Scotland lead automatically to their exploitation? We know that the natural resources of the UK are unevenly distributed, so can we therefore relate uneven development to the uneven geography of natural resources? After all, you cannot have an oil industry without an oil field.

But the reverse is not necessarily true: you can have an oil field without an oil industry.

3.1   GREEN FIELDS AND OIL FIELDS

The photograph below is of an oil field in Hampshire in the South East of England; or, rather, it is of the green field above the oil field. Not far away, some five miles from Basingstoke, is Humbly Grove, reputedly the second largest onshore oil field in the UK. The largest is Wytch Farm in Dorset, in the South West of England. Other notable onshore finds in the South include Baxters Copse, Godley Bridge and Palmers Wood in Surrey, as well as Bottoms Copse on the Isle of Wight, an extension of the Dorset oil field. With names that have the ring of the Countryside Commission about them, rather than any association with the tough North Sea oil industry, these oil fields are nonetheless part of a vast basin of oil that stretches from Dorset to Kent. And this is only one of four main basins in the country. The other basins are in central Scotland, in the East Midlands, and in the North West region around Cheshire. Figure 3 gives you some idea of the geography of the UK's onshore oil resources. To date, over a quarter of the UK is covered by licences for oil exploration or production, with more than a hundred oil companies involved. Clearly, the oil is there. But will it be exploited? And, if it is, will its exploitation lead to the development *of* these regions or development *in* these regions? These are major questions. Let us take each in turn.

A potential oil field in Hampshire

To open up the first question we need to know more about what turns a raw material beneath the soil into a natural resource. With any raw material, this transformation occurs when it is *used* by people. This may sound straight-forward, but it is a more complex point than it may first appear. For a material such as oil to be used, certain social relations have to be in place: certain social pre-conditions have to be met. We can see this more clearly if we look briefly at the history of onshore oil production in the UK and then at the specific case of the oil beneath Wytch Farm.

Not that long — in fact little more than a century — ago, oil seeps in UK coal mines were regarded as a significant nuisance. At the turn of this century and in the years leading up to the First World War, oil shales in Scotland were producing about as much oil every year as the whole of the Middle East at that time (an amount which, by today's standards, is not great). Onshore oil

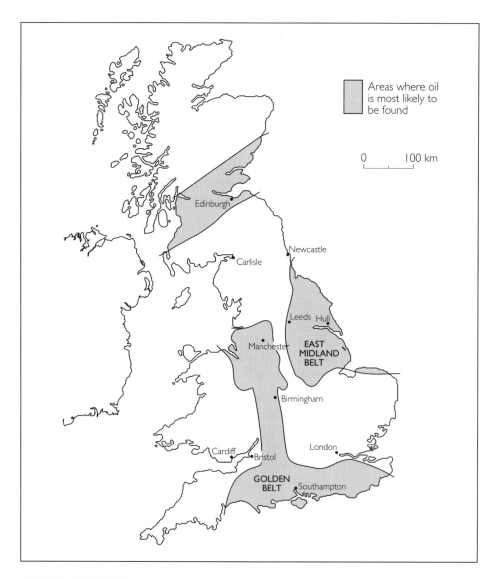

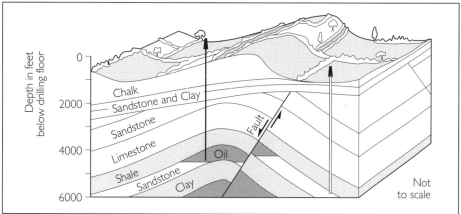

Figure 3   The UK's main onshore oil-yielding areas (top) where folding of the rock layers (above) may have created oil traps deep below the surface

Source: *Money Matters*, 29 September 1985

exploration started just after the First World War, that is, some forty years before drilling commenced in the North Sea. Yet it was not until 1939, in the East Midlands basin, that oil finds of any note were registered. In comparison with the oil fields that were to come on line in the North Sea in the 1970s, however, they were tiny, and it was not until 1973 that the first onshore find of any real significance was identified at Wytch Farm in Dorset. Even so, this oil find was still small compared to those of the North Sea. In 1988, however, the discovery of a large offshore extension to the Wytch Farm oil field fed speculation that the overall size of the field may be equivalent to, or even greater than, the next generation of North Sea fields coming on line. This would set the level of recoverable oil in an extended Wytch Farm at around five hundred million barrels — a sizeable amount even by US standards.

So why should an enlarged Wytch Farm that includes onshore and offshore oil deposits appear attractive to exploit? The size of the find suggests that the field may be potentially profitable to exploit, but not in isolation from at least three pre-conditions.

The first pre-condition is that the technology to exploit the resource is available. If, for example, the oil beneath Wytch Farm is so deep that present technical knowledge is not sufficient to extract it, then that oil will remain an untapped resource — that is, until the necessary technology becomes available, which may be never. For there can be no assurances concerning the speed with which technology may develop, or the direction it may take. Known resources, then, will be classified as inaccessible if the level of technical knowledge for their exploitation is inadequate. In short, such resources would be in the 'wrong place' — for the moment at least.

In the case of Wytch Farm, however, the oil does appear to be in the 'right place' at the right time. Preliminary offshore tests indicate that the oil reserves are accessible with current technology, while onshore, in the words of one of British Petroleum's project managers, 'technically the development is a doddle'. Also, the cost of exploiting the oil field is relatively low. Onshore oil wells cost around one tenth of those in the North Sea and those offshore have had their costs lessened by the availability of appropriate technical know-how developed in the North Sea fields and elsewhere. So, technology is not a brake on the development of Wytch Farm. But neither is technology alone sufficient to guarantee the field's development. There is another pre-condition, which is that a demand for the oil exists.

At first sight this condition appears to have been met. In the early 1990s, oil is a major source of energy for the nation and it is also a significant aspect of the UK's export economy. Without oil, it is often said, the UK's balance of payments (the difference between the nation's exports and imports of goods and services) would deteriorate further. Once again, however, these are not guarantees or assurances. The demand for oil is bound up with the demand for other energy sources, especially coal and nuclear power. Sharp rises or falls in the price of one — whether at home or abroad — will affect the demand for the other two. A sharp rise in the price of oil, for example, may lead to its substitution by either coal or nuclear power. Intervention by the state may also produce a substitution effect. A political preference exercised by a government for nuclear power over, say, coal may lead (as it did in the 1980s) to disused resources and the closure of coal pits, with subsequent job losses in the mining communities. A state subsidy for one resource rather than another can produce a similar outcome. So too, can an effective energy-conservation policy. All in all, there are no hard-and-fast rules which say that if a natural resource exists, and if its deposits are not exhausted, there will be a demand for that resource. At the time of writing, however, the level of world prices and the 'national interest', as defined by the Thatcher government's third administration, both indicate a demand for the oil beneath Wytch Farm.

In short, the technology is available and a demand is acknowledged to exist for the exploitation of the Wytch Farm oil reserves. The same is also true of a number of prospective oil wells in the Home Counties. So will the coming decade see the growth of a number of 'little Aberdeens' in the South?

There is one further pre-condition to resource-use to consider. You may have guessed it already, and the UK oil industry is certainly aware of it. Consider the following point. The designation of an area as being of 'outstanding natural beauty', or as a national park or a nature reserve, is often connected closely with a particular underlying geology — a geology which, it would appear, is also often designated as being of oil-yielding status. Wytch Farm and its surrounding area, in common with many locations within the southern oil basin, is a site of 'outstanding natural beauty', with a variety of unique habitats. Part of the Wytch Farm site, for instance, contains a bird sanctuary and three national nature reserves. Consider then, the possible reactions to the arrival of the oil industry and its associated infrastructure; to increased commercial traffic, pipeline construction, 'nodding donkeys' (oil derricks), rail links, and the possibility of oil pollution — each of which may threaten the local environment. One reaction is likely to take a political form — namely, environmental conflict, or, as in this instance, a clash between two very different kinds of natural resource. These two resources are, on the one hand, a landscape of natural beauty which holds an amenity value for the local population and visitors; and, on the other hand, a landscape of natural minerals which holds a commercial value for those who exercise control over it — in this case, the oil companies and the State. And this takes us directly to the third pre-condition of resource use: that the power exists to control and exploit the resource.

The extension of the oil field at Wytch Farm and the development of wells in the south east corner of England are about relationships of power. These entail a conflict between different uses of nature and, also, between different representations of nature. Whereas a free market economy would ensure that as much oil flowed as possible, an environmentally 'green' market economy would strive to keep the landscape as green as possible. For the former economy, nature is something 'out there' — something to be exploited and controlled; whereas for the latter, nature is essential to everyone's quality of life and should therefore be conserved and enjoyed. And whether the oil comes out of the ground in the South or not will depend, in part, upon the ability of the different interest groups involved — local residents, conservation groups, the oil companies, and government — to persuade people, to mobilize others around their representations of nature. What is more, the outcome of such conflicts will vary from one part of the country to another.

In the East Midlands oil basin, for example, oil companies have met little resistance to the extension of their onshore exploration for oil. With a long history of coal pits and factories, industrial areas like the East Midlands are less likely to view the activities of oil companies as any more disfiguring or disruptive than what they are used to. Compared to those of the coal industry, the development and production methods of the oil industry can be seen as positively environmentally-friendly. Moreover, the oil industry does bring jobs with it. These are admittedly few in number compared with many other heavy industries, but they are nonetheless jobs that are welcome in the older industrial areas.

Another possible dimension to consider when weighing up the different uses and representations of nature is that of nature as a provider of work (through the oil industry). However, this sense of nature is not always received positively. The South East, for example, with little tradition of heavy industry outside of greater London, with a class structure skewed towards the middle class, and, presently, with a problem of too much growth, is likely to see the oil industry in a more negative light. Places (or rather the people who comprise

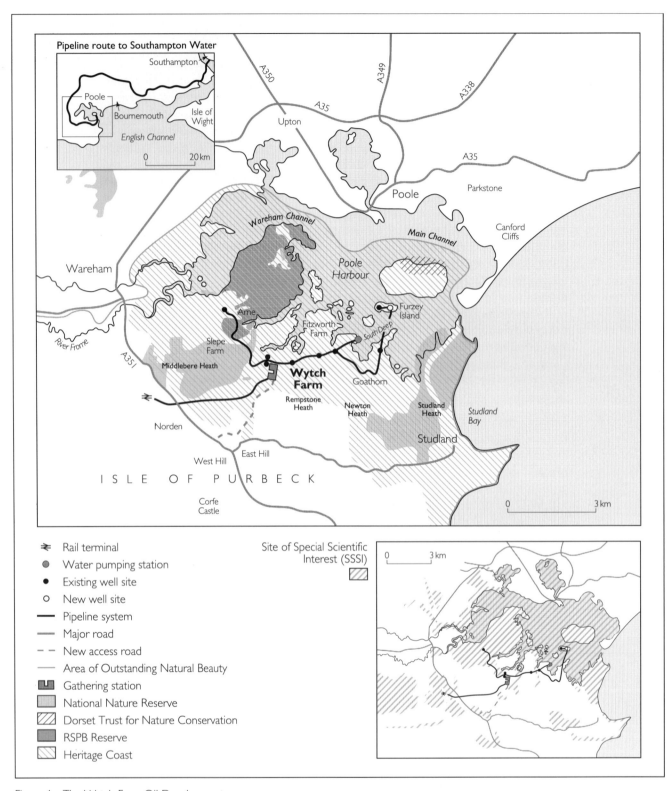

Figure 4   The Wytch Farm Oil Development

Source: *Geographical Magazine*, January 1989, p.19

them, as the last unit spelt out) are also able to shape and mobilize around their own representations of nature.

We are now in a position to give an answer to the first major question, namely, whether the oil beneath the UK mainland would be exploited? From the foregoing discussion, we now know that the presence of oil creates only the possibility of its exploitation. The existence of oil deposits at certain onshore

The Wytch Farm Oil Development
Source: *Geographical Magazine*, January 1989, p.19

locations need not lead automatically to the development of an oil well. Such development depends, as we have seen, upon three pre-conditions: that the technology exists to extract and use the oil; that there is sufficient demand for the oil (at the right price); and that the power to exploit and use the oil is present (a pre-condition which carries its own political geography).

There was a second major question which followed on from the first: If the onshore oil in the regions is pumped out, will it lead to the development *of* or to development *in* those regions? In short, who will benefit?

Certainly the individual landowner is well rewarded, although not to the extent that perhaps you would have thought. If, one morning, you strike oil in your back garden (or window box), your enthusiasm is likely to be qualified. Unlike in the United States, all oil and mineral rights in the UK belong to the Crown. About the best that a landowner can hope for is a lucrative lease with an oil company for the use of the land, and compensation for noise and disturbance. Oil companies, ranging from multinationals to small UK firms, who show a keen interest in the onshore fields can expect better returns. Considerable profits can be achieved from the low-cost, low-accumulation fields. The government of the day also benefits through the collection of petroleum revenue tax. So what does the regional population stand to gain? There are a number of aspects to consider.

First, there is the issue of jobs and what is referred to as the 'regional multiplier'. If we take the example of the Grampian region, centred on Aberdeen, we can get some idea of the economic impact of oil resource exploitation in a region. Clearly, the Grampian region, and Aberdeen especially, has benefited from the considerable number of jobs that oil has brought to the North East of Scotland. These jobs fall under three different headings: direct employment, oil-related employment, and total oil-dependent employment. Direct and oil-related employment refer to jobs connected specifically with the organization and running of the industry, from oil exploration and platform maintenance to helicopter operators and catering contractors. Total oil-dependent employment includes the first two categories, plus the jobs generated in the regional economy through the spending power of the oil workers and oil companies. By the late 1980s, some 53,000 jobs in the Grampian region — around a quarter of the region's total workforce — were attributable to direct and oil-related activities, with the majority in the Aberdeen area. Over five hundred firms in the region depend wholly on the demands generated by the oil industry. Add this job figure to the income multiplier for the industry, and you have an approximate figure of 75,000 jobs that are dependent upon the North Sea oil industry.

The figure has risen swiftly. Since the end of the 1960s, the Grampian region has been transformed from a relatively depressed economy to the fastest growing region in Scotland. And, according to one source, the Grampian Regional Council, the oil industry will continue to generate local growth throughout the 1990s and into the next century. So who has benefited from this growth in the region? How have the economic benefits been distributed across the region? Is this an example of development *of* the region or of development *in* the region?

———————————————— ACTIVITY 2 ————————————————

As you will recall from the previous section, the value of the distinction between development *of* and development *in* a region is that it allows us to make some broad statements, rather than construct detailed calculations. Nonetheless, it is possible to compile a rough balance sheet for the oil industry in the Grampian region based on a few indicators. In this activity, I would like you to consider whether the evidence overall indicates development *of* the region or *in* the region.

Consider the following:

(a) The growth of an oil industry in the region has led to an increase in average earnings, especially for men. The upward pressure on wage rates has, however, made it difficult for traditional industries in the region to compete for labour.

(b) Since the early 1970s, the housing stock of the region has increased by about one third, consisting mainly of private developments. However, high house prices and a falling stock of public housing have created problems for the local population in terms of access to housing.

(c) The oil industry has brought about an improved level of private services, especially hotels and restaurants, and has led to better road and rail communications with the rest of the UK. But it has also brought with it potential environmental hazards associated with the oil industry.

(d) Finally, as noted earlier, oil has increased job opportunities in the region. Many of those employed in the industry reside in the region, although the majority of offshore employees are resident elsewhere in Scotland and northern England (and commute on a weekly or fortnightly basis).

(Information provided by Grampian Regional Council, Department of Physical Planning.)

What does the evidence in (a)–(d) suggest, then, about the kind of development that has taken place in the Grampian region? As in the case of Swindon, it would appear that some social groups have benefited considerably, while others have not. Moreover, some of the benefits appear double-edged: for example, the oil industry provides jobs but it also carries potential environmental risks. Overall, the impact of the oil industry in the Grampian region is mixed; it has led to both development *of* and *in* the region — how you perceive it depending upon who you are.

The impact of the oil industry has not stopped at the borders of the Grampian region. Through offshore work, such as platform construction, and the establishment of oil terminals, the industry has benefited the local economies of the Shetland Islands, Glasgow and even places as far south as Sunderland in the North East of England. Oil benefits, however, are double edged. The improved prospects that oil spin-offs can bring to a local economy can be cancelled should the industry go into recession — as it did in 1986 when world oil prices fell.

Economic swings of this kind, which have a local impact and yet are global at source, raise a more general point about the dependence of regions upon a natural resource. Consider a situation in which a regional resource is far from exhausted, but the resource requirements of the UK economy or the global economy change. Oil has certainly given the Grampian region an economic advantage relative to other regions within the UK, but the scale at which the comparative advantage of a resource such as oil operates is global rather than local. What happens elsewhere in the world economy, in the Middle East for example, or in Japan (which has no oil resources to speak of, and is a major importer of oil), will affect development in the North East of Scotland. Any changes in the value of oil or other energy sources will also influence events in the oil belt that runs beneath the South East of England for some years to come. The particular fortunes of some places, then, are tied to one another.

Natural resources, such as oil and other minerals, are not, however, the only kind of regional resource in which a comparative advantage may be established. One certain resource is people; another is history.

3.2 PAST RESOURCES AND PRESENT RESOURCES

If many of the natural resources of an industrial UK are no longer appropriate to the needs of an emergent service and information age, we should not assume that their commercial use is exhausted. Many resources still possess an economic value. But not, perhaps, in the role that springs to mind when, for example, you think of coal in the Rhondda Valley, or iron workings in the Black Country, or even the dock areas and waterfronts of industrial cities like Glasgow, Liverpool, Manchester, Newcastle, Bristol and parts of East London. For these resources — or, rather, many of the sites of these resources — have been given over to a new economic use: tourism and leisure.

Unit 23 spoke of the growth of Heritage Centres which serve to remind us of a region's past productive role. In some of these places, a worn industrialized landscape has been transformed into a tourist attraction. The past can then be experienced as recreation. Black Country World in the West Midlands, for example, offers a slice of early eighteenth-century industrial history, with a choice of five sites, each representing a different aspect of life and work at a time when iron and iron-working played a central role in the development of an industrial economy.

There is more to this kind of development than simply a replacement of the old by the new. The past resources of an area, and how they were worked, have been endowed with new meanings. The past has, literally, been 're-presented'. To visit Beamish Open Air Museum, a reconstructed pit town on a green field site in the North East, or the Black Country Museum, or the Heritage Centre at Wigan Pier, is to encounter a certain image of place: one that has been sanitized of the harshness and deprivation of past working lives. Until relatively recently, many of the old centres of industry have tried to brush aside their industrial past; now, it is a case of repackaging the past as a tourist attraction. On what used to be the remains of past industries and their resources, we see the rise of new services — the tourist and leisure industries — which are increasingly becoming key aspects of local economies rather than side-shows.

Another way of thinking about these changes is to see the distinctive history or character of places as something that is built up over time, through the succession of roles that those places have played in the wider national and even international economies. As the character and form of the global economy change, so too do the fortunes and prospects of the regions. This, as the previous unit spelt out, is one of the ways in which uneven development is produced. Under one form of global interdependence, the economic resources of a region may generate growth; under another form the very same resources may hinder development. Looking at the UK's heritage industry, we can see that a potential barrier to development — an industrial past — has been transformed into a commercial asset. A new and growing sector of the UK economy — tourism — has responded to an inherited economic geography by taking advantage of a pattern of uneven development laid down a century or two ago.

Much the same can be said for the leisure industry, which has expanded through, among other things, the transformation of 'redundant' water spaces into leisure spaces. Cafes, restaurants, marinas, or pleasing adjuncts to new property developments are all part of this transformation — a transformation which alters nature's function from a resource for producing materials flows to a resource for producing recreation. Ironically, the potential for onshore oil production in areas of 'outstanding natural beauty' in nature conservation areas and the like, would, if realized, take natural resource use in the opposite

Beamish Open Air Museum

direction. Later, we will take up the idea that industry uses existing patterns of uneven development, or rather the accumulation of differences between places, to achieve locational and competitive advantage. For the moment, I want to remain with the topic of resources and regional development, and to move towards a broader notion of regional resources — one that includes labour.

There are a number of good reasons for entertaining this broader view of resources and regional development. One is the economy of the South East. However potentially oil rich it may be, the growth and dominance of the South East in the national economy owes little to the exploitation of its natural resource base. Since the eighteenth century, London and the South East have developed for the most part on the basis of international trade and finance, and, more broadly, as a regional service economy. At the hub of the South East is the City of London, a financial and commercial centre, specializing in international investment, banking, securities and insurance. Its influence however, does not stop at the borders of the Square Mile; the economies of the City and of Greater London shape the pattern of employment and growth in the South East. And they have done so for more than a century. As TV12 and the last unit pointed out, when the fortunes of the northern and midland industrial regions fluctuated in response to global economic shifts, the economies of the City and much of the South East continued to expand and prosper. Even the loss of an Empire failed to deflect the City from establishing and maintaining itself as one of the three contemporary global financial centres, alongside New York and Tokyo. So, what lies behind this 'success story'?

It is conceivable that the City owes its continued prosperity to its physical geography; that is, to a time-zone location that enables City brokers to trade, in the same working day, with New York and Tokyo while both these markets are still active. If so, then this particular advantage may be construed as a 'natural' one. Alternatively, the success of the City may be attributable to the accumulated expertise, to the financial 'know-how', of its workforce and its established formal and informal networks. This is a view which suggests that no other regional centre in either the UK or Europe has a comparable labour force, nor the international skills, or communication networks that London possesses. And if correct, it may be one of the reasons for the growth of US and Japanese banks and finance houses in London (the latter especially since the late 1970s).

We can take this line of enquiry further in relation to other cities and regions. If people and skills are important resources for the financial services industry in London, are they not also important elsewhere in relation to other industries? We could, for example, point to the availability of highly skilled, technical labour along the M4 Corridor and around Cambridge as the reason for the development of research and development industries in those areas. Equally, it could be argued that the jobs that left the inner cities for the suburbs and the peripheral regions in the 1960s and 1970s did so in response to the advantages that companies could gain by employing an available, cheaper supply of semi-skilled or unskilled labour. And if we accept that labour is an important resource in the pattern of growth, does it follow that labour is also bound up with the decline of certain areas? Think about whether the loss of jobs and industry in many inner cities, and in some cases whole regions, has had anything to do with the type of people living there. Did the available workforce lack certain skills? Or did they price the cost of their labour too high? Alongside questions of natural resources and regional development, there is a further set of questions that have to be opened up if we are to explain regional growth and decline.

SUMMARY

Three general arguments were outlined in Section 3. These were:

- First, that the presence of a natural resource does not automatically lead to its exploitation. For example, the existence of coal in a region does not necessarily mean that it will be mined. There are certain pre-conditions: the technology to exploit the resource has to be available; there has to be a demand for the resource; and the power to control and exploit the resource has to be at hand.

- Secondly, that the benefits of natural resource exploitation do not necessarily pass to a region's population. A resource may, for example, be worked to the benefit of local people, or to the benefit of multinationals based outside the region; alternatively, the gains may be realized disproportionately by a central state. There are a number of possible permutations, including an uneven social distribution of benefits within a region.

- Thirdly, that a natural resource may be 'worked' in a variety of ways. For example, a region's natural resource endowment may be mined, or re-packaged and 'sold' as a representation of a past production process. The resources of a region may therefore perform different roles over time depending on the wider national and international context.

4   EXPLAINING REGIONAL INEQUALITY

So far we have considered the role that resources perform in the process of regional development. We have seen that the role that such resources play is not straightforward. It is not possible to conclude that some regions have developed solely because they possess ample resources, whether natural or social. To draw an assessment it is necessary to consider something of the wider economic, and indeed political, context of which they are a part. However, the wider context is itself open to interpretation, and explanations of regional change are often based on divergent views about the *connections* between regional resources and regional inequality on the one hand, and the operation of market forces in a capitalist economy on the other.

As signalled in the Introduction, the intention in this section is to explore the ideas and theoretical concepts that underpin three explanations of regional inequality: neoclassical, cumulative causation, and marxist. First, however, to obtain a broad sense of what each explanation has to say about the nature of regional development, it will be useful to map out their main lines of disagreement.

4.1   MAPPING THE DEBATE

Imagine that you are present at a public debate on regional inequality in the UK. It is a three-cornered debate at which each side in turn has an opportunity to outline its case before spelling it out at length.

(a) The first to speak are members of the *neoclassical* school, who put the following case:

- They point to the economic gap between the regions of the North and the South and claim that such inequalities are not exceptional.

Disparities in, say, regional unemployment rates or wage levels will even themselves out in the short run. The operation of market forces, if left to themselves, will reduce such disparities over time.

- They argue that there is an underlying tendency towards the equalization of regional fortunes. So, for example, if high unemployment in the North forces wage levels below those in the South, then capital investment (in the form of factories and offices) will flow into the North in search of higher returns. And the same set of circumstances will trigger a process of labour migration as workers seek higher wages in the South. With capital tending to move in one direction and labour tending to move in the other, the general drift is towards an equalization of both profits and wages across the country.

- The key phrase here is the *drift towards equalization*. In practice, the neoclassicists would argue, an equalization of regional fortunes does not occur, since the adjustment process does not work in a mechanical fashion. The process of uneven regional development is closer to the way that a see-saw shifts its balance: first, one region will develop at the expense of another, then, as the balance is shifted the pattern is reversed. So, regional inequality is not something to be concerned about. It is, after all, necessary to the efficient operation of market forces in that it is part of a self-correcting process.

(b) To which members of the *cumulative causation* school reply:

- That they enjoyed the elegance of the reasoning, but that in practice market forces do not work like this. Rather than evening-out the inequalities between regions, the play of market forces tends to increase them. There is a cumulative process of development at the heart of all this. For example, once Aberdeen and the Grampian region started to develop, then the very catalyst of growth, the oil industry, generated further growth. An initial advantage conferred further advantages on the region through the multiplier effect.

- So, once economic development in a particular region has begun, instead of a self-correcting process of regional balance coming into play, a self-reinforcing process of growth sets in. Once the demand for goods and services within a region starts to rise, this promotes a shift in investment and a movement of labour away from the less advantaged regions towards the growth regions. The apparently inexorable growth of the South East region is a case in point. The movement of capital and labour, then, is one-way: from the poorer regions to the richer (and increasingly richer) regions.

- For that reason, the image of regional development offered by the neoclassical school is misleading. Regional development is not like a shifting see-saw, but more like a downward spiral of continuing disadvantage (a 'vicious circle') for declining regions, and an upward spiral of continuing advantage (a 'virtuous circle') for expanding regions. The underlying tendency, then, is not towards the equalization of regional fortunes, but rather *towards a polarization of regional fortunes* — the very opposite of what the neoclassical position proposes.

(c) And, finally, in response to both these positions, the *marxists* set out their views:

- They argue that neither the neoclassicists nor the exponents of the cumulative causation view have quite grasped the point. All this talk of development as an equalizing process or as a self-reinforcing process of growth indicates a misunderstanding of the nature of regional development. Development is not merely concerned with spatial inequalities in the distribution of factories, of offices or of workers. It is also about the kinds of investment and the types of jobs that occur in different regions; it is about why 'screwdriver' assembly plants tend to locate in peripheral regions, why research and development functions tend to be found in the South, and why most of the larger UK firms have their head offices in the South East. In short, development is about how industry seeks out the best locations for profitable production.

- That sounds rather abstract. Let's put it another way. Firms 'use' space, and one way in which they may do so is by splitting up the tasks of production and control and locating them in different parts of the country. Strictly speaking, it is not space that is being 'used', but rather the existing pattern of uneven development that is being used. So, for example, one of the reasons for the location of a Japanese car assembly plant in the North East is because of the type of labour available — relatively cheap and compliant. To an incoming multinational, the North East represents a profitable place. In this way, capital 'uses' the regions, including their inherited past to maintain the process of capital accumulation.

- The result of this spatial division of labour is a rather complex economic geography, one that produces *a pattern of regional inequality that is continually changing*. There is nothing irreversible about cumulative growth; nor is there any predictable see-saw process of regional development. Wrecked regions may turn themselves around on the basis of a new set of economic activities. Some regions may experience decline for long periods, even centuries. There is no easy predictability; only the secure knowledge that not all regions can be 'winners'.

We will leave the debate there. You should now have an understanding of the *broad differences* that separate the three accounts of regional inequality. Before we go on to a lengthier treatment of each explanation, it is worth noting one feature of the debate. This is that some kind of meaningful communication between the three positions *does* take place. True, some of that communication is on the basis of misunderstanding. Even so, there is more than a hint of theoretical engagement: an engagement over the priority of certain concepts and their interpretation. This is the very stuff of theoretical controversy. Later, in Unit 26, we will take up the important issue of how to choose between the three explanations and how such an assessment may be conducted. Moreover, in that unit we will also look at how each of the explanations has, in different ways, been influenced and shaped by wider traditions of thought. For the moment, however, we will focus on their contributions to the debate over geographical inequality.

4.2 NEOCLASSICAL EXPLANATIONS

From a neoclassical standpoint, the power of competitive markets — the unhindered operation of market forces — is all that really needs to be considered. According to this view, it is the mechanisms of supply and demand which ensure that the balance of development shifts from region to region. Declining regions cannot decline endlessly, nor can growth regions expand in perpetuity. In this respect, neoclassicism is at odds with the cumulative causation view that the balance mechanism of the scales of development is fixed.

History, the neoclassicists would argue, lends support to their interpretation of regional change in the UK. Economic development since the early Industrial

Revolution in the eighteenth century has seen a succession of regional economies taking the lead, often on the basis of a handful of industries. And the emergent dominance of a region is usually accompanied by the relative stagnation of others. This pattern of regional history should strike a familiar chord. It does, after all, appear to fit the pattern of regional development described at the end of the last unit:

> The early Industrial Revolution saw the rise of Lancashire (and also Shropshire and the Black Country). The later importance of steel, coal, railways and ships brought with it growth in south Wales, the North East of England and central Scotland. The period from the end of the nineteenth century until the inter-war years saw another pattern again. This was the age of imperialist expansion *par excellence*, and this time the leading regions were the West Midlands and Greater London whose strength was based on the new electric power and synthetic materials. From the Second World War until perhaps the 1970s (there is debate about this), the leading industries in the economy were predominantly geared to domestic consumption, and the new industries were based on such technologies as electrical engineering. Again it was the West Midlands and Greater London which benefited. While new industries grew apace in these areas many regions in the North went into long-term decline, forming one element of the North–South divide we know today.
>
> (Unit 23, Section 4)

A see-saw process of development can also be gleaned from the process of job decentralization discussed briefly in Section 2 of this unit. There we noted how jobs moved out from the cities as firms attempted to escape the economic disadvantages of inner-city locations, namely, the high cost of land and premises, city congestion, and an expensive, well-organized workforce. From all this, the neoclassicists can point to a reasonable degree of 'fit' between their interpretation of regional growth and the evidence. And what lies behind regional growth — the causal momentum at work — is, they would argue, strictly neoclassical in form.

In other words, it amounts to shifts in the supply of and demand for capital and labour between the regions in response to the appropriate price signals. And it is this play of market forces that produces the tendency towards the equalization of regional fortunes — in so far as employers and workers strive to achieve the 'best' outcome for themselves. We have seen why this kind of see-saw development should be the dominant pattern. At its simplest, it involves the migration of capital and labour between rich and poor regions.

For example, wage levels in the South East of England are at present higher than wage levels in the northern regions. This may be attributable to labour shortages in the South and labour surpluses in the North. Competition between firms for labour in the South East is likely to have pushed up wages, whereas unemployed workers in the northern regions have to 'price' themselves into the labour market by accepting a cut in wages. Or, as the neoclassical model suggests, they will migrate to the South East. If they do so, they will be achieving the 'best' position for themselves, and be responding to a market signal which tells them that higher wages are available in the southern economy. A similar 'best' position is available to firms in the South East; this would take them to the northern regions to take advantage of cheaper labour costs.

Of course, it is recognized that this kind of market adjustment — the movement of workers out of low wage regions and the flow of capital into them —

will not happen overnight. There are time lags involved. Nonetheless, it is assumed that people will migrate and that firms will move in response to the price signals which tell them in which regions the best returns, in wages or profits, are available. And, as the regional price signals change — for example, as the level of unemployment decreases in the North in response to the opening of new firms and businesses — then so too will the price of labour change: wage levels will rise and the initial advantages to an incoming employer will diminish. Eventually, capital will flow out of the region towards those regions which offer better returns on investment. The balance of the development scales will shift and once again the regional 'see-saw' will change position. We can consider the empirical support for the argument by looking at the migration trends in Table 1.

Table 1   Regional migration, 1965–1986

	Migration 1965–79		Migration 1979–86	
	(000)	(%)[1]	(000)	(%)[1]
South East	−247	−2.6	104	1.0
South West	198	8.5	123	4.8
East Anglia	154	16.1	49	4.3
East Midlands	74	3.4	26	1.1
West Midlands	−52	−1.7	−57	−1.8
Yorks. & Humberside	−90	−3.1	−36	−1.2
North West	−125	−3.2	−102	−2.6
North	−110	−5.7	−47	−2.4
Wales	−52	−3.2	−4	−0.2
Scotland	−298	−9.5	−101	−3.1
Northern Ireland	−104	−12.2	−30	−3.4
United Kingdom	−652	−2.0	−71	−0.2

[1] Migration as a percentage of the population of working age.
Source: Smith, 1989, p.173

───────────────────── ACTIVITY 3 ─────────────────────

Table 1 shows the pattern of regional migration over a twenty-two year period. You should note that this is only one indicator of a potential adjustment process, albeit an important one for the neoclassical argument. Taking each of the two periods shown in turn, I would like you to decide whether a labour market adjustment took place between the regions in either period.

(a) Take the period 1965–79 first and cast your eye down the list of regions. Make a note of which regions gained and which regions lost population through migration. Is the period one that is characterized by a process of labour market adjustment between rich and poor regions?

(b) Do the same for the period 1979–86. In what way does the pattern of migration differ from the earlier period?

───

The first period is rather difficult to interpret with any degree of certainty. It is clear that only three regions gained: the South West, East Anglia and the East Midlands.

However, it is more difficult to chart the direction of migratory flow. To my mind it would appear that the outflow *from* the South East boosted the numbers in the adjoining regions. If this is indeed the case, then clearly the late 1960s and 1970s do not provide a straightforward example of North–South migratory flow. The evidence suggests a more complex pattern of migration flows.

The second period provides us with a clearer pattern. We can see that in the first half of the 1980s only four regions registered a net gain in migration. (Note that three of these four regions together constitute the South.) On this evidence, it could be argued that the 'price signals' for labour were working relatively efficiently; that is, the price mechanism was conveying the necessary information for people to decide where the 'best' use of their labour could be obtained. (Although the figures do not tell us what kinds of workers migrated or for what reasons.)

In comparison with the late 1960s and 1970s, therefore, it can be argued that the early 1980s provide an example of labour market adjustment in operation. And, if the assumption of the model is correct, we could anticipate that at a later date there would be a reversal of this flow.

In this simplified account of the neoclassical position much of the detail has been put to one side so that the key features of the balancing mechanism can be identified: the mobility of capital and labour in response to market price signals. Other factors which would undoubtedly affect the balancing mechanism — such as the existence of highly unionized workforces in certain regions, the impact of new technology upon skill and employment levels in different regions, or the variation in population growth between regions — are part of the bundle of things left to one side. If they were to be included in the working model as qualifying assumptions, then the ability of the model to produce uncluttered, precise predictions would be weakened. And for the neoclassicists, as noted in Unit 11, this is an important consideration, in that the predictive power of a model is identified with its explanatory power. (We will return to the issue of explanatory power in Unit 26.)

So how accurate is the neoclassical model in accounting for uneven regional development? As we have seen, there is some degree of 'fit' between a 'see-saw' view of development and the shifting fortunes of different regions. Are we then to assume that the free play of market forces is the causal power responsible for the 'see-saw' pattern? This is more difficult to accept. In practice, neoclassicists recognize that market mechanisms alone are not likely to even out regional differences in wage levels and profitable returns. National wage agreements in industry, the collective power of the trade union movement, the regional inequities in the operation of the housing market, major public investment decisions (the channel tunnel, for example), and the presence of formal and informal networks in certain locations (as in the City) may each create obstacles to the free play of market forces. And if real wages remain high in areas of high unemployment then this is the result of market imperfections, such as when large firms set wages at a national rather than a local level, or when the labour movement exercises excessive power in those areas. Equally, if the central state should embark upon a major infrastructural project in a growth region, creating growth on top of growth, the price signals for labour and materials are likely to distort, and thus disturb the self-correcting process. Similarly, the sheer cost of establishing the formal and informal networks of communication that are in part responsible for the City of London's success is likely to prove a serious obstacle to other cities and regions wanting to emulate this pattern of growth.

It could be argued, therefore, that one of the reasons why regional inequalities remain is precisely because vested-interest groups continue to interfere with the free workings of the market. Another related reason could be that the markets are not generating the right kinds of information to bring about a regional adjustment. People do not move simply in response to relative wage levels; and firms do not have to move out of their own regions to reduce overhead costs and achieve labour savings. Nonetheless, neoclassicists would argue that an underlying tendency towards the equalization of regional fortunes is still in operation, although its effect has been blunted. The implication is that the adjustment mechanisms of an *unimpeded* market would 'take out' the regional imbalances. In other words, the returns to capital and labour between the regions would tend to equalize.

4.3 THE CUMULATIVE CAUSATION SCHOOL

If we were to identify the one characteristic of the neoclassical model that separated it from the view held by the cumulative causation school, it would be the assertion that regional fortunes have a tendency to equalize. According to Myrdal (1957), whose arguments are at the centre of the cumulative causation school, regions generate advantages for themselves over time. Capital investment in a region will lead to a higher level of economic activity in that region, and this will in turn attract further capital for investment. Workers will respond to these boom conditions by moving from the depressed regions to the more prosperous regions. As the title of this school of thought indicates, the process is a cumulative one. Once a region takes the lead, the initial development promotes further growth and economic success becomes to some extent self-reinforcing. The scales of development may not be rigged, but they are certainly weighted.

It is at this point that we have to consider again the evidence on regional change in the UK. After all, in the last sub-section we noted that there was a reasonable degree of 'fit' between the neoclassical interpretation of regional development and the historical evidence. Think again of the historical sketch at the end of Unit 23 which identified *different* regions as being at the core of successive waves of economic development. Is it possible for both accounts — the neoclassical and that put forward by Myrdal — to be correct? In fact, on closer examination the cumulative causation school point to a different piece of evidence — a very different geography. After the historical sketch in Unit 23, we were reminded of a constant feature of the UK's changing regional geography: the dominance of the City and the South East in the UK economy over the last two hundred years or more. This point was also mentioned in Section 3.2 of this unit. It has been expressed forcibly by Lee (1986):

> The continued growth of the South East in the present century, latterly spreading into East Anglia and the South West to form an enlarged and very prosperous southern economy, has been mainly based on the expansion of those employment sectors which constituted its growth before 1914. Employment decline has been modest because the region did not have very much of its employment vested in those sectors which have contracted in the twentieth century, except for clothing and domestic service. This regional economy has not, therefore, had to contend with the restructuring on a massive scale which has been necessary in many other regions. Traditionally, the economy of the South East has been oriented towards services and consumer goods centred on the national capital which was a major centre of international trade and finance, seat of government and fashionable society.
>
> (Lee, 1986, pp.263–4)

It can be argued, therefore, that over a two century period the South East region has reinforced its position as the 'core region' of the UK economy. As a centre of international finance and commerce, and boosted in recent years by Eurodollar business, the South East's economic lead can perhaps be regarded as secure, even unquestionable. And, interestingly, this pre-eminence is once again attributed to the play of market forces across the regions.

However, according to Myrdal, market forces, if left alone, will *increase* the inequalities between regions. This outcome, as indicated earlier, is the reverse of that predicted by the neoclassical model. There are a number of steps to the argument. First, in so far as economic growth does not take place evenly across the country, nor at the same pace, an initial locational advantage, if success- fully developed, is sufficient to trigger the process of cumulative growth. A locational advantage can take a variety of forms, ranging from the presence of natural resources to the existence of certain kinds of labour in a region. If we consider this last point in the context of our earlier discussion of resources in Section 3.2, then the City's accumulated expertise — the financial 'know-how' and tradition of its workforce — can be seen as a locational advantage: an historical advantage that perhaps corroborates Myrdal's view that success will generate further success. Moreover, if we accept the logic of this view, then it follows that poorer regions without a tradition of such advantages are less likely to attract industry. Regions which fall behind in the initial stages of development are thus likely to experience great difficulty in closing the eco- nomic gap. Once behind it is difficult to catch up, especially as the advantaged region is still moving forward. (You may recall a similar argument about cumulative processes of uneven development in Unit 2. There the reference was to the inequalities between nations; here we see that a similar argument can be made for regional inequalities within a nation.)

The second step in the argument is that the favoured regions will be further favoured by the *regional multiplier effect*. This effect was mentioned in Section 2 in the discussion of what development is. In brief, the idea of the multiplier effect is that growth multiplies itself in the following way. Growth generates demand for goods and services in a region. The greater the numbers that are employed in a region the higher the spending, especially if they are high- income earners. Likewise, the bigger the expansion of industry in a region, the greater is the demand for locally produced commodities. This attracts firms to exploit that demand, which in turn leads to an increased demand for labour and thus to a further expansion of markets, and so on. And the faster the pace of regional growth, the faster is the pace of productivity growth and technical innovation. The implication is that economic activity will concentrate in cer- tain regions which, over time, will develop the status of 'core regions'.

An important feature of these 'core regions' is that they will generate the positive benefits of economic activities clustering together. As regional centres expand, the proximity of workplaces, housing and shops allows easy access to a range of goods and services. Transport networks evolve to serve the central locations, and the time-and-money costs of distance are further reduced. Furthermore, a greater share of health and educational services will be provided to meet the needs of an expanding population. Regional centres are in this way another kind of activity space in which various economic activities are integrated, although each may possess a geography that reaches beyond the region. The Grampian oil industry for example, is as much tied into the multinational space of US oil corporations, as it is tied into the local economy of the Shetlands.

The third step in the argument is an important one in that it binds together the economic fortunes of expanding and declining regions. As in the neoclassical account, there is a zero-sum dimension to the argument. Once regional growth has begun, the dynamic is sustained by the inward flow of capital and labour from the peripheral, less advantaged regions. The poorer regions tend to lose their better-qualified workers to the 'core region', thereby reducing further the likelihood of attracting investment to themselves. Moreover, the faster productivity growth at the core creates a series of competitive advantages which make it increasingly difficult for the less advantaged regions to compete in the market-place. Their attempts at industrial development are undermined by a flow of goods from the core which stifles what little industry has emerged. The benefits accruing to the expanding region are therefore at the expense of development at the periphery. Myrdal refers to these aspects of regional inequality as the 'backwash effects' of core growth upon the periphery. The flow of labour migration from the North to the South (noted earlier), for example, could be construed as part of a 'backwash effect', especially if the majority represent skilled workers. Hirschman (1958), writing soon after Myrdal, refers to the same phenomenon as 'polarization effects'.

Regional development is not regarded as a simple zero-sum game, however. There are counteracting influences. At a certain stage of development at the core, the 'backwash effects' are offset by 'spread effects' which carry the momentum of growth to other regions, especially those that are linked by means of markets to the core. The assumption is that economic growth will radiate out to the regions. Thus, it is possible to view the boom conditions in the South East economy as beneficial to the rest of the country — as something that will benefit the whole country, eventually. From this standpoint, the expansion of the South is potentially a good thing for the North.

In practice, the counteraction of the 'backwash effect' and the 'spread effect' is a matter of empirical observation. Certainly, a pattern of regional divergence is considered to take place before any kind of growth turning point is reached. And Myrdal is insistent that the two 'effects' never reach some kind of balanced position, whereby each cancels out the other. The broad picture he paints is one of regions becoming less equal over time. A region is rich because it is rich. A 'virtuous circle' of growth works for the advantaged regions, whereas a 'vicious circle' of decline operates in the less favoured regions. If the South East economy is a growth-pole, then its success is achieved largely at the expense of the peripheral regions. Note, however, that this development is not necessarily at the expense of growth in the regions closer to the core, in the South West, East

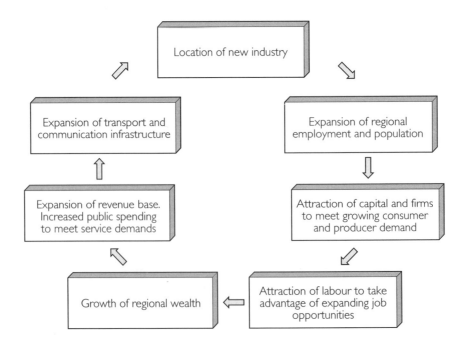

Figure 5   The process of cumulative causation (steps 1 and 2 simplified)

Anglia, or parts of the Midlands, and even certain locations in south Wales. In each of these places there is some evidence of 'spread effects' in operation. To take just one example in the 1980s, a number of banks and insurance companies, including the Bank of England, moved part of their service operations from the South East to the western regions. (It is also worth thinking again about the regional migration data in Table 1. Was the period 1965–79 an example of 'spread effect'?)

4.4 MARXIST EXPLANATIONS

A common feature of neoclassical and cumulative causation approaches is the stress that they place on the role of market forces in shaping the pattern of uneven development. From a marxist standpoint, this emphasis upon market movements is simply misplaced. Uneven regional development is taken by marxists to reflect something deeper — something more fundamental to the way in which the UK economy is organized. Harvey (1982), for example, wants to emphasize the *capitalist* nature of uneven development, urging that the uneven geography of the UK is a necessary feature of the way in which a capitalist economy works and changes over time. For Harvey, uneven development is something that is built into the very operation of the system.

At its simplest, the marxist account suggests that regional inequalities take their shape from the class inequalities in economic power. Regional inequality in this context is something that is produced and used by industry to maintain a competitive advantage. Regions, or rather regional labour forces and their qualities, are used when it is possible and profitable for industry to do so, and discarded when they no longer satisfy the conditions for profitable production. The class character of different regions — the past and present balance of class forces in each region — therefore enters into the account. In this kind of explanation, what is important is not the scales of development or the balance mechanism, but rather who owns and controls the scales.

Part of the marxist argument is that the pattern of regional inequality shifts continuously over time, with each new pattern creating the pre-conditions for a subsequent pattern of uneven development. As a description of regional development this view fits neither the 'see-saw' model nor the 'core–peripheral region' model. Yet in one sense, the marxist description could be stretched to fit either model simply by pointing to particular regions at particular moments in history: the dominant role of the North East at the end of the last century, based on coal and shipbuilding, and the subsequent decline of both industries; the success of the West Midlands' engineering-based economy from the 1930s until its collapse in the late 1970s; the more recent growth of the 'sunbelt' industries in parts of the South West region; or even the continued acceleration of growth in the early 1990s of the service-based economies of London and the South East. These can all be explained by a rather loose view of shifting inequalities between regions. But it is not the *pattern* of regional inequality that concerns marxists; rather it is the *form* of regional inequality that is of interest to them.

According to Massey (1984), the form of uneven development changes over time in response to broader changes both in the wider economy and in the division of labour. Uneven development, in this argument, has its roots in the unequal division of labour in society and how that division is organized over space. In Unit 1 you were introduced to the notion of an international division of labour, whereby people in one part of the world specialize in the production of certain commodities, whilst in another part of the globe a different set of commodities is in the making. This is one form that a *spatial division of labour* may take.

The first two examples of regional economies above — those of the North East and the West Midlands — depict a 'sectoral spatial division of labour'; that is, the form of uneven development in which different regions specialize in one or, possibly, two industries. This element of sectoral specialisation works in the same way for regions as it does for nations. In the first few decades of this century, distinctive regional cultures were part and parcel of this regional specialization and, in many ways, so too were regional class structures, with a number of firms owned and controlled by local capital.

Today, much of this regional specialization in the UK has broken down, and marxists would argue that a new form of uneven development has emerged in response to changes in the wider division of labour in society. A new spatial division of labour is said to be in place — one which reflects the changed organization of production in certain industries and the class relations that characterize those industries. It is not that capital investment alone is unevenly distributed over space or, for that matter, the number of jobs; also unevenly distributed are the different tasks of production and control within industry.

Within a number of manufacturing and service industries, the routine production work has been separated spatially from the tasks of management and control, and from those of research and development. Those people who plan and control the geography of investment and the location of jobs are highly concentrated in the South and East of the UK, where many of the head offices of leading UK companies are located. Similarly, highly skilled scientists and technologists tend to cluster as a class in the outer South East and in the semi-rural locations of the South West, forming part of the growing 'sunbelt' economy. In contrast, the northern regions have a greater proportion of their workforces involved in the tasks of direct production. From all this, marxists argue that the geography of class is in the process of being redrawn. Regional class structures are beginning to derive their character from different parts of the production process, rather than from one or two industries.

We can get a clearer idea of these arguments by looking at the distributions shown in Tables 2 and 3. The evidence offered in Table 2 is fairly unambiguous, in that it confirms the dominance of London and the South East as a centre of strategic control in the economy. Of the one hundred largest firms in the country (including a number of foreign-based firms), eighty-nine have their headquarters in the South East, and especially in London.

Table 2   The 1987 head-office location of the UK's top 1,000 companies, by region

Companies by ranking	London	Rest of SE	South West	East Anglia	East Mids	West Mids	Yorks./ Humber	North West	North	Wales	Scotland	Northern Ireland
1–100	73	16	1	0	1	3	3	2	0	0	1	0
101–200	50	21	6	1	2	6	1	6	2	0	5	0
201–300	39	32	1	2	2	6	6	7	2	0	3	0
301–400	29	33	2	1	6	5	7	6	1	2	7	1
401–500	29	28	1	3	6	8	11	7	1	0	6	0
501–600	27	34	2	1	6	5	8	9	2	2	4	0
601–700	24	36	4	4	6	3	5	9	3	1	5	0
701–800	38	22	3	1	7	7	9	5	0	0	7	1
801–900	24	23	3	4	7	8	8	8	4	2	8	1
901–1000	21	25	4	4	7	10	11	7	4	1	6	0
1–1000	354	270	27	21	50	61	69	66	19	8	52	3

Source: Smith, 1989, p.224

Table 3 Occupational grouping in the UK of persons aged 16 or over, 1987

	Total in employment[1] (percentages)	In employment						Self-employed	Unemployed or economically inactive	Number of persons (thousands) =100%
		Employees								
		Managerial and professional	Clerical and related	Other non-manual	Craft and similar	General labourers	Other manual			
South East	59.5	16.5	11.1	4.1	5.8	0.2	12.8	8.3	40.5	13,597
South West	56.7	12.7	8.3	4.8	6.5	0.2	14.3	8.9	43.3	3,627
East Anglia	57.6	13.2	7.4	5.2	7.5	0.4	14.9	8.2	42.3	1,576
East Midlands	56.5	11.8	7.5	3.7	9.9	0.5	15.2	6.7	43.5	3,097
West Midlands	55.0	12.5	7.4	3.8	8.5	0.5	15.3	5.7	45.0	4,067
Yorkshire & Humberside	54.3	11.9	7.0	3.8	8.0	0.5	15.4	6.2	45.7	3,849
North West	53.9	12.7	7.9	3.5	7.4	0.4	14.3	6.0	46.1	4,974
North	52.6	11.5	7.2	3.8	8.2	0.6	14.4	5.0	47.4	2,422
Wales	48.5	10.6	5.9	3.4	6.9	0.6	13.4	5.9	51.5	2,226
Scotland	52.1	12.0	7.0	3.7	7.4	0.3	15.5	4.6	47.9	3,991
Northern Ireland	49.6	9.4	8.0	3.2	6.5	0.4	12.8	7.9	50.4	1,128
England	56.7	13.9	8.9	4.0	7.2	0.4	14.1	7.2	43.3	37,211
United Kingdom	55.7	13.4	8.5	3.9	7.2	0.4	14.1	6.9	44.3	44,557

[1] Includes those on government employment and training schemes, employment status not stated and occupation not stated/inadequately described.

Source: *Regional Trends*, vol. 24, 1989, HMSO

In many ways it is difficult to draw firm conclusions from the quantitative evidence presented in Table 3 as the kinds of arguments made in this section rest largely on qualitative, case-study evidence. Disentangling the different types of economic activity that make up each occupational grouping is not an easy task, given such a broad descriptive classification. Nonetheless, it is possible to generalize from this kind of evidence. For example, it looks as if many of the occupations that we associate with routine tasks and low paid employment are disproportionately concentrated in the northern regions; and, conversely, it seems that much of the management and control work is concentrated in the South East. Although the pattern is open to more than one interpretation, it is certainly possible to argue on the basis of this evidence that an *intra*-sectoral spatial division of labour between regions has emerged, or is emerging.

For marxists, regions are also losing their shape in a related way as new industries, both national and multinational, use the existing form of spatial inequality to maintain a competitive edge. As the previous unit suggested, the coherence of south Wales as a region has been fractured, first by the decline of the coalfields and, more recently, by the arrival of the branch plants of foreign multinationals. To some extent, the old and the new forms of the division of labour co-exist — although one is rapidly disappearing and taking with it much of the distinctive working-class character of the region, whilst the other is progressively softening class divisions. More importantly, this new wave of inward capital investment and the types of jobs that it brings with it are taken to represent the new 'role' of the region in the wider, international economy. And this idea of regions performing 'roles', or rather a succession of 'roles' over time, is a key factor in Massey's account of uneven development.

Briefly, Massey argues that certain regions, by virtue of their past economic character, may hold new attractions for incoming firms like multinationals.

One attraction, for example, would be the availability of a 'green', female labour force (discussed earlier in Section 2) in locations like South Wales or other peripheral regions. This would depend upon the particular locational requirements of an incoming multinational, and whether or not it was establishing production in a country to seek, among other things, this type of 'green' labour. Other types of multinational — for instance those involved in research technologies or scientific developments — may be attracted to a different kind of region because of its highly skilled, technical workforce and its clustering of research and development activities. The locational requirements of industry vary, as do the attractions that regions hold for industry. The 'old' industrial regions, for example, with their worn landscapes, may now be at a disadvantage compared with those regions which 'missed' the Industrial Revolution (unless, of course, they are able to transform their past into a tourist attraction). Yet with each new 'layer' of capital investment, Massey argues, a new form and pattern of regional inequality is laid down.

MISSING THE INDUSTRIAL REVOLUTION
WAS A BLESSING FOR THE IRISH

There is one further strand to this argument. If different regions, or parts of regions, perform different roles in a wider division of labour, then it is not possible for every region to play the same role at the same time. For every 'sunbelt', there have to be other locations that carry out the tasks of producing things. One set of economic activities is dependent on the other, so that the two locations are interrelated. It does not follow that the two sets of activities have to take place in the same country, but equally it is unlikely that all regions of a country will be busily involved in, for example, high technology research. The success of the M4 corridor is not something that can be multiplied across the country — at least not at the same time. The same would be true of the financial success of the City. In that sense, inequality between regions is something that is built into the process of regional change. If the division of labour in society is unequal, then that inequality is also *structured* across space. It follows that a zero-sum mechanism is also a feature of this type of explanation.

SUMMARY

Three explanations of regional inequality were examined in Section 4:

(a) The neoclassical approach

- The central idea of neoclassical accounts is that regional inequalities will tend to even out if market forces are allowed to operate freely.

- In this way, the price signals of the market act as a self-correcting process, 'taking out' regional imbalances and redirecting resources between regions in a more efficient manner.

(b) The cumulative causation school

- As the title of this school indicates, regional advantages are seen to accumulate rather than even out. Once ahead, a prosperous region will stay ahead.

- Again, it is the market that is regarded as the causal mechanism, although for this school the workings of the market increase rather than decrease inequalities between regions.

(c) The marxist view

- The general view advanced by marxists is that geographical inequalities are not just the result of market forces, but are integral to the way capitalism works.

- Therefore, regional inequality is something that is produced and used by industry in the search for profitable investments. As the nature of the broader national and international economy changes, so too does the role played by different regional economies.

ACTIVITY 4

You have now worked through three main explanations of regional inequality and considered some of the main differences between them, together with a few significant points of overlap. In a moment we will return to the three questions asked about uneven development in Section 2 to consider the answers that each explanation would offer to these questions. But before we do so, you should spend a few minutes reading the short description of your region in the extract entitled *Regional Economic Prospects — To the Year 2000*. As you can see from its title, this extract forms part of a report which projects regional economic trends to the year 2000. Now think about the following questions.

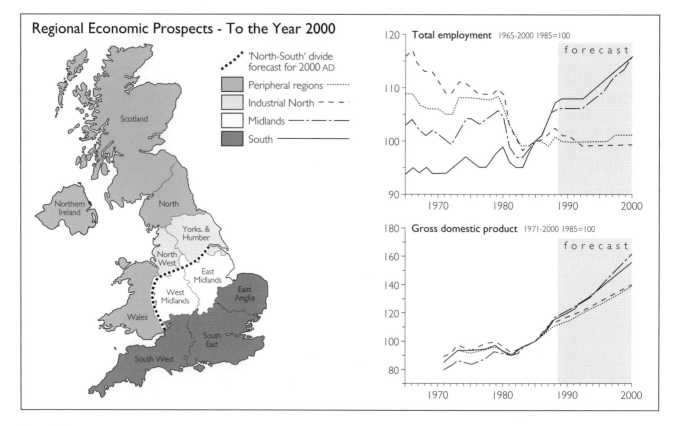

South East

The rapid expansion enjoyed by the South East throughout the 1980s is forecast to slow down in the 1990s, due mainly to a shortage of labour. Even though the region will receive an economic boost from the Channel tunnel, a further crossing of the Thames at Dartford and expansion at Stansted and Luton airports, congestion, increasing house prices and higher salaries will syphon off growth to neighbouring regions. Employers will be encouraged to decentralize and invest in more and more labour-saving technology. Growth is projected at 2.1 per cent a year between 1990 and 1995 and 2.3 per cent between 1995 and 2000, compared with national rates of 2.3 and 2.6 per cent respectively. Unemployment is predicted to fall below 5 per cent. But there will be a heavy shake-out in manufacturing with the loss of 225,000 jobs offset by 550,000 new jobs in government and private services. By the turn of the century eight in 10 jobs in the region are expected to be in services, transport and communications.

South West

The environmental attractions and relative prosperity of the South West will result in the region's population swelling by 800,000 to 5.4 million by the turn of the century — a good proportion of that increase made up by migration from other areas. This will increase the size of both the working population and the labour force. Healthy growths in output of between 3.5 and 4.3 per cent a year will create almost 500,000 new jobs, predominantly in the service sector. But the growth will not be evenly spread. Most of the Bristol area, east Dorset (with its service, marine and electronics industries), and Exeter and Taunton will fare well. But in the depressed south-west of Cornwall, already sporting high unemployment and ravaged by the decline of tin mining and tourism, the picture is less rosy. Much will depend on whether enough land is made available in Plymouth and Bristol to maintain the influx of manufacturing companies and allow for spin-off high-technology developments.

East Anglia

East Anglia, the most sparsely populated region of England, is forecast to stay at the top of the regional growth league over the next decade achieving an increase in output almost double the national average. On virtually every index of prosperity — from employment and consumer spending to quality of life — the region will stay comfortably ahead of other areas. It is also one of the few predicted to enjoy a growth in manufacturing where an extra 40,000 jobs will be created. But employment in the two sectors traditionally associated with this sprawling rural belt — agriculture and food — will actually fall. Growth is forecast to be intense around Cambridge where technological output from the university will spawn new businesses. Although the population will grow to close on 2.5 million, fuelled by a continuing inflow of retired people, labour shortages will be a constraint on growth and researchers expect planning restrictions to be relaxed to allow a surge in house building.

North

The North region, taking in Cumbria, Northumberland, Durham, Cleveland, and Tyne and Wear, is forecast to suffer the same vicious circle of declining employment, weak growth and low consumer demand as the North West, only less severely. By the turn of the century the region will have lost another 50,000 jobs leaving it with an unemployment rate three times that of the South East. The advent of 1992 is forecast to leave the North even more peripheral to the heartland of the European Community, a trend exacerbated by the boost to development that the Channel tunnel will provide in the South. Doubling of output from the Nissan car plant will not offset the run-down of, or job losses in, shipbuilding, heavy engineering, chemicals, mining and steel. There will be a net increase of only 11,000 jobs in the private service sector, and widening regional wage differentials will further dampen consumer spending. By the year 2000, the North's population is projected to have dropped below 3 million for the first time since the 1940s.

West Midlands

The West M lands, once the engine room of Britain and now having emerged from the ravages of recession to stage a modest recovery in manufacturing, is more firmly ensconced in the 'southern' half of the UK. However, the next decade will see the region treading water with virtually no increase forecast in employment or population. The service sector, which has been the focus of growth in part-time and self-employment, will continue to outperform manufacturing. The key features of the region are likely to be a growing homogeneity between the economic performance of its sub-regions and a growing divergence from the national average performance. Manufacturing employment is predicted to continue falling as greater automation comes to the traditional engineering and car industries. Growth will fall to just below the national average. The number out of work will fall until the early 1990s, then rise through the middle part of the next decade, and then fall again.

East Midlands

Although one of the less urbanized regions of the UK, the East Midlands has consistently enjoyed a buoyant economy and the remainder of this century will be no exception. It provides a sharp contrast with its near neighbour, the industrialized West Midlands. The ability of the East Midlands to continue expanding may have something to do with its curious mix of affluence, as measured by the proportion of high-income earners, and average wages which are among the lowest in the UK. During the last five years of the century unemployment is forecast to drop to just 2.6 per cent across a region which extends from the farming belt of Lincolnshire to the traditional textile and footwear county of Leicestershire. Total employment is expected to rise by 20 per cent but manufacturing employment by only 6.3 per cent. Output is forecast to increase at a rate of 4.2 per cent between 1995 and 2000. Population is forecast to rise by more than 600,000 to 4.6 million.

Yorkshire and Humberside

The key to the fortunes of Yorkshire and Humberside may well rest with the success of ventures to redevelop its older industrial and urban centres. In Sheffield, which sports an Urban Development Corporation along with Leeds, schemes worth almost £2bn are under development to regenerate an area hit by the decline of the steel industry. But as many of these involve retailing, much depends on future levels of consumer spending — this is forecast to grow at less than half the rate of the mid-eighties. Although output is only projected to grow at about the UK average and employment in basic manufacturing to decline by some 40,000, the region will have the lowest unemployment rate outside the Midlands and South of England. Skill shortages and the lack of a developed electronics base may stunt growth. The north of the region is forecast to enjoy more buoyant conditions than the urban conurbations of the south and west. Population is forecast to grow 1.7 per cent to just under 5 million.

North West

The outlook for the North West is almost wholly depressing. It is forecast to fare the worst of any UK region, suffering the biggest fall in employment, output growth barely half that of the national average and a growing exodus of the population. By the end of the century the region is projected to have lost 222,000 jobs — representing a fall in its share of national employment from 10.1 to 8.8 per cent. The textile, clothing and footwear industries will be virtually decimated; 50,000 jobs, representing a fifth of the workforce, will disappear in engineering

alone. The region will not even have the solace of increase demployment in the service sector where 51,000 jobs in the public and private sectors will go. This will lead to growing migration of the working population, from 7,000 a year in 1988 to 13,000 a year by 2000, and a collapse in consumer spending which will grow at only a quarter of the national rate. Pockets of affluence and economic buoyancy will remain — notably Cheshire. But despite the attempt to breath new life into Merseyside through initiatives such as the redevelopment of Liverpool's derelict docklands, the possibility of an economic miracle in this area remains remote. The one hope for the region is that it may gain through decentralization by firms in the South East seeking cheaper locations and investment by local entrepreneurs.

Wales

Of all the 'peripheral' regions, Wales, the second smallest in Britain, is projected to fare the least badly. Employment and overall growth rate will expand towards the end of the century, but the Welsh economy will still underperform that of the UK as a whole through the mid 1990s. It is the only region likely to reap benefits from its proximity to southern and midland England. Much will depend, however, on the region's ability to erase its reputation as a declining heavy industrial area and to continue attracting foreign investment as coal mining and, to a lesser extent, steel contract. If an extra 5,000 jobs beyond those projected were created each year, employment growth in Wales would be maintained at the national average up to 1995 and increase the population by 75,000. If this does not materialize, unemployment is expected to remain above 10 per cent — equivalent to a slight fall in employment compared with the 1.7 per cent increase expected nationally.

Scotland

Scotland is projected to enjoy two years of modest boom until the bubble bursts in 1990 and both employment and output growth start to lag behind the UK average for the rest of the century. The region's unemployment rate is expected to peak at 12.9 per cent in 1991 and then fall to 7.6 per cent by 2000. Most sectors of Scottish manufacturing — notably steel, where British Steel's Ravenscraig integrated works is under threat — electronics and food are forecast to underperform counterparts elsewhere in the UK, resulting in 70,000 job losses. A return to higher oil prices could create 10,000 jobs, but these would not offset the decline of the coal industry where productivity will fall sharply along with deep-mined coal production. Scotland's population is forecast to fall a further 132,000 by the end of the century and consumer spending per head is projected to remain a consistent 6.6. per cent below the UK average.

Northern Ireland

Unemployment in Northern Ireland, the smallest and most depressed of the UK's regions, is forecast to rise through the 1990s, reaching 20 per cent by 2000 even thought the number of jobs will remain static at 564,000. This is because the labour force and population will continue to increase at a pace which outstrips available jobs. Some 33,000 jobs will disappear in manufacturing, construction and agriculture, but government and private services will take on 34,000 employees. Recent successes in attracting foreign investors may need to be offset against the long-term threat hanging over the province's two biggest employers — shipyard Harland and Wolff and aerospace company Shorts — and the danger that escalating political violence will deter expansion. By the year 2000, manufacturing is expected to account for 15 per cent of employment and 20.8 per cent of output, compared with national figures of 18.2 and 26.7 per cent respectively.

Source: *The Independent*, 3 January 1989; based on a report by Cambridge Econometrics

(a) Which of the three explanations of regional inequality examined in Section 4 do you think underpins the report's assessment of regional trends?

This is the 'big' question and you will need to read two or three of the regional extracts to get a broad enough idea to answer the question. Avoid spending too much time on the actual statistics. Instead, you should focus upon whether the general drift is towards a pattern of regional equalization or towards a pattern of regional polarization? Or does the report suggest that the pattern of regional inequality will vary up to the end of the century?

(b) When you have broadly decided which kind of explanation is guiding the analysis of regional prospects, jot down the theoretical 'signposts' that led you to your conclusion.

What I have in mind are the *key concepts* or *major assumptions* of an explanation which inform the overall assessment, rather than the actual projections. Section 4.1 on 'Mapping the debate' will be of use to you in recognizing these aspects, as will the above summary. We will return to the issue of how explanations are put together in Unit 26.

(c) Think about the types of evidence, quantitative and qualitative, presented in Sections 4.2, 4.3, and 4.4 respectively. What kinds of evidence are used in the report to justify its assessment. Which of the explanations (neoclassical, etc.) draw upon similar types of evidence?

(You will find my observations on this extract at the end of the unit.)

5   UNEVEN DEVELOPMENT AND UNEVEN ANSWERS

I now want to return to the three questions asked about uneven development in Section 2 and explore the answers that might be given to them by the three approaches examined in the previous section. We will take each question in turn.

Question 1: If the North–South divide is so distinct, why are 'local' divides within regions often felt more sharply?

Earlier it was suggested that there is no straightforward answer to this question. It was recognized that different economic processes throw light upon some lines of geographical inequality and not on others. And it was acknowledged that certain processes of growth or rapid decline may therefore either exacerbate intra-regional differences or decrease them. Everything depends upon the precise nature of the global processes at work and their local variation, as well as how the changes are explained.

For example, all three approaches that we have looked at agree that industry will be attracted to certain locations and that a complex rather than a simple economic geography is characteristic of the UK. But there is lack of agreement over the processes behind that geography and where the lines of division should be drawn. True, there is some agreement between the neoclassical and the cumulative causation schools over the central mechanisms at work — namely, the movement of the markets and the changing price signals for capital and labour across the regions. But their differing understanding of *how* markets operate inclines the two schools to argue for opposing geographical outcomes. From a neoclassical viewpoint, growth in the South will eventually give way to growth in the North as the markets adjust to the 'overheated' conditions in the southern economy. The line of division, therefore, will shift slowly northwards. For the cumulative causation school, however, the dividing line will remain firmly rooted in the south of the country as the economic gap between the South East and the rest of the country intensifies and widens.

Moreover, as the UK moves towards an integrated European market in the 1990s, it would be consistent for the cumulative causation school to argue that the 'core region' of the South East will shift, as it were, closer to the European mainland. Consequently, rather than attempting to identify the major lines of geographical inequality in the UK, our attention will shift to divisions *within* Europe. In this type of scenario, the South East would be one among a number of European 'core regions', with the rest of the UK as part of a sizeable European periphery.

Indeed, the geographical scale at which an explanation is pitched will influence how we see the unequal geography of the UK working out, and also direct our attention to different social processes. From a marxist position, it is assumed that the uneven pattern of development will shift continuously as industry moves around the UK and the globe seeking out profitable conditions of production. What interests capital is precisely the diversity of social conditions within and between countries at any one point in time. As the conditions of profitable production shift, so too, according to the marxists, will the lines of geographical inequality. In other words, the cumulative causation school may well be correct in their prediction that the South East will 'break away', but not just because of the way that markets work.

The South East may break away to the European mainland

Question 2: Does the success of some cities and regions depend upon the failure of others? Are the fortunes of places linked to one another?

We left this question unanswered in Section 2. Much of the discussion there revolved around two issues: first, the independent or interdependent nature of urban and regional growth, and, secondly, the possibility of there being a fixed sum of development.

Certainly, there is a sense in which all three explanations subscribe to the notion of interdependent development and the idea that a 'zero-sum game' of development is in play. In the cumulative causation account, it is the core regions that develop at the expense of the peripheral regions. In the neo-classical account, the locus of growth shifts back and forth between favoured and less favoured regions as resources move between them. And in the marxist account, the stress placed upon an unequal spatial division of labour, with different parts of the country performing different economic tasks, implies an interdependence of economic activities. Moreover, all three accounts give the impression that the total sum of development is fixed; that is, one region's loss is another region's gain. However, the impression is an ambiguous one. In none of the explanations is it entirely clear that the sum of development *is* fixed.

Take the example of London's Docklands. According to the neoclassical model, it is possible to reproduce the sort of growth that the Docklands has achieved in other run-down inner city areas. If the market is allowed to operate freely, if the barriers to its free movement are removed, then the economic differences between places would begin to even out and places like Glasgow or Liverpool would level up rather than down. In this respect, the pool of development does not appear fixed as this additional growth would not necessarily be achieved at the expense of the Docklands. Thus all places could be seen as 'winners' of a kind. Similarly, the view of the cumulative causation school that growth at the core may spill over into the adjoining regions at a certain stage in the core region's development does not necessarily imply that such 'spread effects' involve costs to the core. Both core and its hinterland may experience growth together. The Docklands development, for instance, may stimulate growth around it. The question that remains, of course, is whether such a growth pole expands at the expense of the further outlying regions.

It is at this point that we need to consider our geographical terms of reference, and to decide whether we are referring to a national sum of development, a global sum, or something in between. Our answer to the above question will then reflect the kind of development that is under consideration. For example, the development of offices and luxury housing in the Docklands is closely tied up with the role of the City of London in the world's financial markets, and so the Docklands' success as an inner-city venture may depend upon the ability of the City to remain the major financial centre in Europe. From a marxist standpoint, there are no guarantees this will happen. Frankfurt, and possibly Paris and Amsterdam, is equally well-placed to perform London's current global financial role, assuming that only one major European centre is likely. In this instance, the 'zero-sum game' has a European boundary. In other cases — for example the electronics industry discussed in Unit 23 — the parameters are world-wide.

Question 3: What is meant by the term 'regional development'? And who benefits from such development?

In dealing with this question, we drew a distinction between development *of* a region and development *in* a region. Development *of* a region, you may recall, referred to a situation in which the majority of a region's population benefited one way or another from economic development. Some might benefit from better job opportunities, others through the economic spin-offs of new industry

The Nissan car factory in Sunderland

moving into an area, and so on. By contrast, development *in* a region may be loosely understood as the absence of these benefits. The value of the distinction is that it alerts us to the possibility that growth is not always positive in its impact. How this distinction is applied, however, is a matter of interpretation.

Consider one of the multinational companies featured in TV12: the Japanese car manufacturer, Nissan. Within a marxist framework, the introduction of a car assembly plant into the North East would be seen to reinforce the 'backward' character of the region as one of low skills and low labour costs. Marxists would argue that it is as if part of the region has been 'contracted-out' to a foreign-owned multinational, to whom most of the economic benefits will flow. The feature emphasized in this type of argument is the location of low-level, routine production work in places like the North East. While the functions of control are located in Japan, the lower rungs of the spatial hierarchy of production are to be found in the poorer regions of the UK. This, marxists argue, should not be seen as regional development, but rather as regional 'use'. When the company no longer requires this kind of regional labour force, it will shift development elsewhere, taking the economic prospects of an area with it.

Thus, in a marxist account, it is an international class of owners that benefits from this type of multinational development. In the cumulative causation account, however, the distinction is drawn less sharply. According to this school of thought, overseas direct investment in a region is certainly one that involves economic risks; yet a number of potential benefits are also possible, ranging from the transfer of technological know-how and the enhancement of skills among the labour force to the much-prized multiplier effects. Indeed, it is quite possible that the location of a multinational branch plant in a region could represent the type of locational advantage which sets up a dynamic of cumulative growth. In this way, a less-favoured region may be able to break out of a vicious circle of decline. Therefore, in this picture of development, the region's population as a whole would enjoy greater prosperity.

Much of this picture also fits the neoclassical sketch of regional development, which predicts that the flow of capital investment will be directed towards the lower cost regions, away from existing centres of high growth. One important difference, however, is that the spread of economic activity from prosperous to less prosperous areas does not necessarily entail a shift towards the equalization of incomes, either within or between regions. From a neoclassical viewpoint, inequalities are a necessary part of a prosperous, efficient economy. They act as an incentive for the less well-off to sell their labour at a low price to firms like Nissan. This is taken as an indication of market forces working efficiently and which, over time, will benefit the North East region and the UK economy as the total output of the national economy grows. In this scenario, everyone is seen to benefit — eventually.

6   CONCLUSION

In this unit, we have devoted considerable time to the issue of how we explain uneven development. In doing so, we have examined some of the potential causes of regional inequality in the UK and have considered why that inequality matters. Above all, we have seen that the inequalities associated with the contours of uneven development are about more than simple geographical differences between places. The fortunes of some regions are tied to others. But this is not the only reason why geographical inequalities matter.

The concentration of economic growth in the South of the country, for instance, matters to the development of the national economy as a whole. As we move into the 1990s, growth in the South East has stretched labour resources there to the limit, whilst in the North people with valuable skills remain unemployed. Those who move to the South hoping to take advantage of the jobs available there find themselves confronted by high living costs and high house prices. Congestion in the South East region has led to calls for further public investment to alleviate an already creaking transport network, at the same time as services and infrastructure in the North operate at below capacity. There are national costs involved in all this: costs of growth, as 'overheating' raises the costs of production, and costs of decline, as resources lie idle or under-used.

Congestion in the South East

The uneven concentration of growth also carries with it a further negative impact. Too much growth incurs environmental costs in addition to economic and social costs. Traffic congestion, industrial pollution, the loss of the country-side — these are some of the external costs of concentrated growth. At the time of writing, we are witnessing the formation of anti-growth political coalitions in the South East which threaten to influence the direction of growth in the region, if not in the country as a whole.

At Summer School, the environmental dimension of uneven development will be explored further. And in the next unit another dimension of uneven development is added to the block narrative: namely, the politics of uneven development. For if uneven development matters economically, it surely also matters politically.

ANSWERS TO ACTIVITY 4

(a)   In my view, the report's assessment of regional trends to the year 2000 is closer to the cumulative causation model than to either of the other two explanations. Although there is certainly a measure of regional equalization forseen, the projection tends to reaffirm the dominance of the South, coupled with beneficial 'spread effects' to adjoining regions (including Wales). It is clear that the authors of the report do not anticipate growth radiating out to all regions over time.

(b)   The handful of theoretical 'signposts' that I noticed were: a reference to a 'vicious circle' in the North; talk of reaping benefits from the regions' proximity to the South (the 'spread effects'); and a general reference to 'peripheral regions', which implies, by contrast, some kind of 'core'. Other than in these cases, it is perhaps interesting to note the generally low profile of theoretical statements in the projection.

(c)   Clearly the projection relies upon aggregate statistical trends for each region, as one would expect in this kind of empirical study. The variety of figures for regional growth, job prospects, migration flows, and population change add up to a fairly comprehensive picture of regional change, as well as of differences in fortune within regions. What is missing is any kind of qualitative assessment of regional prospects, but it is perhaps unrealistic to expect such assessment in this type of study. Of the three explanations examined in Section 4, I would have said that those of the neoclassical and the cumulative causation schools have greater confidence in this kind of numerical data. We will look at this issue more closely in Unit 26.

REFERENCES

Bassett, K. *et al.* (1990) 'Economic and social change in Swindon' in Anderson, J. and Ricci, M. (eds) *Society and Social Science: A Reader,* Milton Keynes, The Open University.

Harvey, D. (1982) *The Limits to Capital,* Oxford, Basil Blackwell

Hirschman, A. O. (1958) *The Strategy of Economic Development,* New Haven, Yale University Press.

Lee, C. H. (1986) *The British Economy since 1700: A Macroeconomic Perspective,* Cambridge, Cambridge University Press.

Martin, R. (1988) 'Industrial capitalism in transition: the contemporary reorganization of the British space economy' in Massey, D. and Allen, J. (eds) *Uneven Re-Development*, London, Hodder and Stoughton.

Massey, D. (1984) *Spatial Divisions of Labour,* London and Basingstoke, Macmillan.

Myrdal, G. (1957) *Economic Theory and Undeveloped Regions,* London, Duckworth.

Smith, D. (1989) *North and South: Britain's Economic, Social and Political Divide,* London, Penguin.

ACKNOWLEDGEMENTS

Grateful acknowledgement is made to the following sources for permission to reproduce material in this unit:

Text

'Regional Economic Prospects — to the year 2000', first published *The Independent*, 3 January 1989.

Tables

Table 1: 'Regional migration, 1965–1986', and *Table 2*: 'The head office location of Britain's top 1000 companies, 1987', in *North and South* by David Smith (Penguin Books, 1989) copyright © David Smith 1989; reproduced by permission of Penguin Books Ltd; *Table 3*: 'Occupational grouping of persons aged 16 or over, Spring 1987 by region', *Regional Trends 1989*; reproduced with the permission of HMSO.

Figures

Figure 2: 'Changes in manufacturing and service employment 1971–1987' Martin (1988), Department of Employment; (note: revised figures to 1984 are now available); *Figure 3*: Crace, J., 'A new bonanza on land', *Money Matters*, 29 September 1985, Australian Press Services Pty.

Photographs

p.61: British Nuclear Fuels, plc; *p.64*: Edwin Smith; *p.72*: BEAMISH: The North of England Open Air Museum; *p.86*: Mary Evans Picture Library; *p.93*: Nissan; *p.94*: Environmental Picture Library.

UNIT 25   FROM UNITED KINGDOM TO UNITED EUROPE?

Prepared for the Course Team by Allan Cochrane

CONTENTS

1   INTRODUCTION

1.1   UNEVEN DEVELOPMENT AND POLITICAL CHANGE

This block focuses on the local-global theme of the course, approaching it in different ways in each of the units. Previous units have stressed the importance of *uneven development* in helping to understand the direction and nature of contemporary change in the UK. Unit 23 started with cultural developments, exploring some of the ways in which places are made and make themselves. One of the central concerns of the unit was to explore the implications of uneven development at the international level, and to place the UK and its localities within a wider international context. Local experiences need to be understood in the context of global changes. Unit 24 was more concerned with uneven development within the UK, showing how regional inequalities are generated and reproduced. It discusses the processes of uneven development which help to generate uneven patterns of growth and prosperity.

Both units look at economic factors, exploring the crucial changes which seem to underlie wider shifts and rearrangements within British society. They show how the UK is geographically fragmented between regions and localities, to the extent that their links to other agencies in the international economy are often of more significance to their development than any links within the UK. TV12 highlights some of the different ways in which involvement with Japanese investment has affected development in the North East of England and the City of London. It is increasingly difficult to justify an approach to economic change which focuses on a national economy, since international (or global) processes cut across arbitrary national divisons to directly influence and interconnect with activity at regional and local levels.

This unit will take some of the insights developed in the earlier units further by looking more closely at political change within the UK, setting it within the framework of changes taking place at the European level. In politics as well as culture and economics, the interaction between the local and the global is vitally important. But it is not possible to 'read off' political change directly from economic change. Politics is a rather more messy and less predictable process. As we shall see in looking at post war developments in the UK, identifying pressures and tendencies is one thing, but confidently predicting the direction of broad political trends is rather more difficult.

1.2   UNEVEN DEVELOPMENT AND THE STRUCTURES OF THE UK STATE

Unlike most other European countries the UK's very title seems to acknowledge diversity - it is the United Kingdom of Great Britain and Northern Ireland - and even Great Britain covers the three nations of England, Scotland and Wales. By implication, at least, therefore, the significance of uneven development seems to be recognized. Yet institutionally the UK is also one of the most centralized countries in Western Europe. According to one set of commentators in the mid 1980s 'Britain stands in sight of a form of government which is more centralized than anything this side of East Germany' (Newton and Karran 1985, p.129). In the light of events in Central Europe in the early 1990s, presumably the search for a more centralized state would now have to move further east.

Official government statements stress that the United Kingdom is a unitary state, that is one in which power is delegated from above, from the centre (indeed, ultimately from the Crown), rather than one in which it is distributed among a range of institutions. Such statements help to illustrate the continuing power of the conservative tradition within British society. As one government publication puts it, 'We live in a unitary and not a federal state. Although local authorities are responsible to their electorates, they derive their powers from Parliament. Their structure, duties and functions have been subject to frequent modification by Parliament as the needs of the country have changed.' (Department of the Environment/Welsh Office 1983, para 1.2). There have never been statutory guarantees of local government autonomy and self government as there are in some other European countries.

Nor are there elected regional governments in the United Kingdom (although some local authorities in Scotland are called Regional Councils). There are not even elected governments for any of the 'nations' which together constitute the United Kingdom (at least since the early 1970s when direct rule was introduced for Northern Ireland, and the province's parliament — Stormont — was abolished). The regional offices of government departments in England, and even the separate Scottish, Welsh and Northern Ireland departments are all departments of the UK state with no formal responsibility to the region or 'nation'.

So, uneven development seems to find no expression within Britain's political institutions. They are national (UK) and centralized. Most political discussion in the UK focuses on Parliament and Whitehall. And — although there are some important exceptions with newspapers based in England's regions and, more significantly, in the UK's component nations — this is reflected in the majority of political reporting, in press, magazines, on radio and television, where the details of parliamentary manoeuvring are given far greater prominence than discussion of regional issues or the development of local initiatives. Sub-UK nationalism only forces its way into the headlines of the London based press when there are dramatic by-election results or direct terrorist action has resulted in the destruction of property or people have been injured or killed. Local government generally only makes an appearance when it can be held up to ridicule, for example because a council has granted money to a group considered to be unrepresentative, or an individual appears to have been victimized by unsympathetic council officials.

Despite this dominant view — a powerful ideology in the terms developed in Unit 17 — one of the central arguments of this unit will be that it is impossible to understand some of the key issues of contemporary politics without looking more closely at changes taking place below the level of the UK state. Uneven development is a vital component of political as well as cultural and economic change, and means that it is necessary to look at the interaction between social, political and economic processes in particular places.

The intention of this unit is to develop our understanding of uneven development and the local-global theme by looking at some aspects of post-war politics. The emphasis is on political processes in the UK and their development in a European context. The unit explores the theme by looking at two main issues:

- first, the extent to which, and ways in which, politics is fragmented within the UK at regional and local levels; and
- second, whether new forms of politics are developing which are not orientated towards the UK state, but towards supra-national institutions, such as the European Community.

ACTIVITY I

Before reading further, try to assess (a) with which political agencies you are in most frequent contact, and (b) which you feel have most impact on your daily life. Try to rank (that is, list them in order of) their relative importance.

Political agencies	Contact	Impact
I. Local governments and their departments		
2. National government and its departments		
3. The European Community		
4. Political parties		
5. Community groups/neighbourhood organizations		
6. Pressure groups		
7. Others/specify		

---

2   REGIONS AND NATIONS IN THE UK

The earlier units of the block have emphasized the extent of regional differentiation, but its political significance may seem less immediately apparent. Until the last quarter of the twentieth century, there were few signs of pressure for regionally based political representation. So why was this? And how significant have more recent shifts been?

2.1   BRITAIN IN THE WORLD

At this stage of the block (and the course), it will probably not surprise you to learn that a useful starting point for answering these questions is to set the UK in an international context — to place it within the global system (in this case literally the world system) of which it is (a local) part.

The UK's position within the international system has been of vital importance for its development as a state, particularly since the nineteenth century. This can be seen most clearly in the economic sphere, but the UK's economic position was itself always linked to international political arrangements. This is perhaps most obvious in the growth of the UK's colonial empire, but the international free trade system of the nineteenth century was also a product of the UK's political as much as its economic dominance.

Unit 23 highlights the way in which the Lancashire cotton industry grew and developed as part of a world economic system. Similar processes underpinned economic growth in the country's other industrial regions, which either produced directly for these international markets or underpinned those which did. If they were not producing goods for export, the heavy engineering plants (such as Vickers) were producing armaments to maintain the UK's international position. It is not surprising that the dominant representation of the UK was as workshop of the world. When 'Britain' was 'Great' its regions were 'Great', too. They grew together. They too were externally oriented, exporting their products throughout the world. Through most of the nineteenth century, free trade was the slogan of the regionally based industrial interests as well as the London based financial institutions. There was little scope for, or interest in, the development of a separate regional politics.

But, as James Anderson notes in his Reader article ('The United Kingdom: legacies of the past' pp.11–30), the high point of British economic power had already been reached by the middle of the century, and was increasingly coming under challenge, as new competitors (such as the USA and Germany) began to take on the old producers. Although the UK remained a powerful and prosperous country, and retained a self image which stressed imperial power, by the 1880s the international balance of economic power had already begun to change decisively. In the twentieth century the balance of regional prosperity within the UK shifted to reflect this, as new industries developed in the South East and the Midlands, while the older ones declined in the North of England, Scotland, Wales and Northern Ireland.

The regions of the UK existed within a world system, with direct relations with other parts of that system, but their position within the UK was also important for them. The UK's political role was as significant to them, as the strength of its commercial and financial system. Until 1945, the 'unity' of the United Kingdom was clearly reflected in the interaction between political and economic activity. For much of the twentieth century the position of Britain's regions within the UK was dependent on the existence of the British Empire and the markets associated with it. Between 1870 and 1938 the share of British exports going to countries in the Empire actually rose from 26 per cent to 46.5 per cent, while the share of exports going to Western and Central Europe and the USA fell from 39.3 per cent to 19.9 per cent (Aldcroft and Richardson, 1969, Table 12). The continued existence of these virtually captive markets helped to mask the extent of decline elsewhere. The UK state had a major part to play in sustaining these markets, as well as directly providing demand for some of the traditional industries, including shipbuilding and armaments. So the English regions and non English nations remained dependent on a strong UK state system.

The period *since* 1945, has been characterized by a withdrawal from Empire for Britain, and the need reluctantly to adjust to a new set of rules in the international market place. The state has had to manage a long period of decline, and to adjust to the rise of a new set of dominant political and economic powers on the world stage, particularly the USA, but also Japan and the Federal Republic of Germany. In Chapter 10 of the Course Reader Crafts points out that in terms of its own past performance, the UK economy grew significantly in the postwar period, but compared to the rates achieved by its main rivals, its growth remained weak. The UK faced relative international economic decline, despite experiencing growth in absolute terms. Unit 14 discusses some of the economic and strategic consequences of the diminution of power associated with the withdrawal from Empire and Unit 15 notes the constraints placed on UK politicians in the 1970s by the pressures of the world economy.

The implications of these changes for England's regions and the UK's component nations in economic terms have been relatively clear. The old industries have declined alongside the Empire, and their replacements have either been part of wider international organizations — with home bases in the USA, Japan or Europe — or oriented towards regionally based service provision, particularly through retailing. The City of London — the biggest UK growth sector in the 1980s — continues to play in the world league, but its links to other regions, for example as a source of investment finance, are rather more limited. As TV12 shows, the City needs to be considered alongside the other international centres with which it deals, such as Tokyo and New York, rather than provincial cities, such as Birmingham, Newcastle, Glasgow and Cardiff. And, within an increasingly internationalized sector, it is one player among many, following Wall St. and Tokyo as often as it gives the lead.

SUMMARY

- The UK's regions developed as part of the growth of the UK as a world state. When Britain was 'Great', its traditional regions were 'Great' too.
- The UK state has managed a long period of decline, during which it has developed policies to support these regions, which in turn remained oriented towards that state.
- The traditional regions have declined economically alongside the UK and its Empire.

2.2   THE POLITICS OF REGIONAL DECLINE

The changing shape of regional politics cannot simply be understood through an analysis of changes in the world economy and the UK's position within it. The regions exist within a UK political system whose operation, too, has helped to shape them and with which they interact as 'local' parts of a 'global' (UK) system.

At first, until the late 1970s, the management of the UK's decline as a world economic and political power encouraged a regional politics still largely oriented towards the state in Whitehall. This was the era of regional policy, in which financial assistance was channelled from the centre to major regional investors, towards large scale infrastructure and nationalized industries in the regions. The industries in decline in the regions (coal, steel, shipbuilding, and parts of the car industry) were brought into state ownership, to the extent that Doreen Massey comments that the regions themselves might even be referred to as 'nationalized' (Massey 1984, p.202). The demands raised by regional politics were for more state aid and better state aid. They came from trade unions and the Labour Party as well as representatives of local industry, and the ground rules were accepted across the party political spectrum. The main argument was over which areas deserved assistance and which did not, rather than whether this was an appropriate way to proceed.

As a result the regional economies of the 1990s have been the product of 'political' as much as 'economic' decision making. In this context, it is difficult to sustain a clear cut division between the private and the public. The interpenetration between private decision making and the state makes it difficult to unpick the two. Private decision making on levels of investment was made in the context of an economy whose existence was dependent on the developments of state policy, and state policy was developed in an economic context largely determined by decisions taken within the international market.

The policies of the state were themselves binding together the regions by providing a focus for political alliances within them, encouraging a regional politics rooted in the social reformist tradition, and linked to the ideas of Keynes (summarized in the *Economy and Society* part in Section 2.2 of Chapter 22 of the Course Reader). This was clearest in 'traditional' regions such as south Wales and the North East of England, where there is a long history of regional organizations aiming to lobby government and in some cases to develop their own growth-oriented activities, primarily through publicity seeking to attract inward investment. These regions — and others like them — were first identified as 'distressed areas' in the 1930s. And the identification of a 'regional' problem by the UK state also helped to reinforce their regional identity. Within the regions, alliances developed between state (local and central government), trade unions and major employers around a programme of assistance, focused on the provision of basic infrastructure, subsidies to major corporations and nationalized industries and the attraction of branch plants on industrial estates. During the 'long boom' after 1945 councils in the North — and particularly the North East — of England were in the forefront of attempts to change their image, to construct a new infrastructure, to produce a region of the twentieth century. A whole new world was to be created which could challenge the dominance of London, with the help of new towns, industrial estates, ring roads, motorways, city centre redevelopment and the provision of other urban infrastructure. In other words, despite the tendency to deny the existence of significant political debate outside Westminster, there was an active regional politics of growth and development, even if it was not reflected in electoral politics or formal political institutions.

=============================== READER ===============================

Now read the sections headed 'Politics and labour in Teesside' and 'Experiences of life in Teesside' (particularly the last couple of pages), as well as the concluding comments of Chapter 21 of the Course Reader (pp.228-35). These outline the basis of regional politics in the post-war period and some of the problems associated with it. In particular, you need to consider:

- which groups were involved in the growth alliance;

- which were dominant;

- what their aims and ambitions were;

- how the basis of the alliance has been undermined since the 1970s.

Turning to the last of these questions first, it looks to me as if the basis for regional politics of the sort discussed in Chapter 21 were being eroded after the mid 1970s, not least because by the end of the 1970s almost all of the UK outside the South East was covered by some scheme of regional assistance. Even under the 1974–79 Labour government there was a significant shift away from *regional* policies towards industrial policy and inner city policy. Although Labour's industrial policies did have regional implications, they were directed at specific industrial sectors rather than particular regions. They were explained as policies directed towards the regeneration of British industry. Where successful, they implied a concentration of activity, the rundown and closure of older and less efficient plants, usually at the expense of the traditional regions. After 1978, when the Inner Urban Areas Act was passed, spatially oriented policies were largely focused on the inner cities, with a move towards policies of economic renewal through public-private partnership, and partnership between different levels of government. The 'inner city' problem began to replace the 'regional problem' as a key concern of government policies.

The chapter confirms that the broad political alliances and arrangements which could be identified at regional level in the post-war period were generally based on supporting the existing industrial structures and key players within them, trade unions as well as employers. They were basically defensive, seeking to gain a share of whatever national growth was taking place. But this meant they found it difficult to cope with the sort of economic restructuring which was taking place in the 1970s at international and national levels (and which was outlined in Units 23 and 24.). The ownership of firms bore increasingly little relationship to the regions within which they were based, and there was a remarkable degree of specialization, even within the same firm: to summarize crudely, head offices tended to be located in London and the South East, research (and sometimes development, too) tended to be located in the South and South East of England (outside London), while manufacturing, assembly and (sometimes) routine office work tended to be distributed around the rest of the UK. The precise arrangements varied between industrial sectors and types of firm, but the existence of division along these lines is not in dispute.

Most major employers in the traditional regions were, by the 1980s, either nationalized industries or the branch plants of national and multinational companies. The regions were having to live with the consequences of 'globalization' discussed by Robins in his chapter in the Course Reader (Chapter 19). The implications of this for the development of regionally based 'growth' coalitions were potentially fatal. In the short term workplaces such as manufacturing plants or offices might be spatially fixed, but in the longer term their regional 'loyalty' was bound to be in question particularly where it was financially advantageous to close them and locate production (or other activity) in some other region instead. At the end of the 1970s, economic survival for many UK based and multinational concerns seemed to involve an extensive restructuring in which support for their branches in regions outside the South East did not have a high priority. The major industries in regions such as Teesside on which growth had been based in the past had already been nationalized and were in substantial decline.

The move away from any explicit regional policy accelerated dramatically after 1979. The newly elected Thatcher government brought policies which aimed for national renewal around the slogans of empowering the market and rolling back the boundaries of the post-war welfare state. It was this state itself which was blamed for Britain's economic decline and reduced international status. The key task of the new government was to exorcise the unholy trinity of Keynes, Beveridge and social democracy. This period saw the most explicit political confrontation between liberal and social reformist traditions: in which leading politicians directly referred to key thinkers within those traditions to justify substantial changes of political direction. Hayek and Friedman were mobilized as alternatives to Beveridge and Keynes. One reason for the final rejection of regional policy was, of course, an acceptance of many of the neo-classical arguments outlined in the previous unit by those then making policy, which substantially coincided with the market based liberal approach of the new government.

──────────────────── ACTIVITY 2 ────────────────────

Look back at Unit 24, Sections 4.1 and 4.2. What attitude would you expect neo-classical theorists to have towards policies of regional assistance?

I think they would be highly sceptical, suggesting that less state involvement rather than more would encourage appropriate readjustment between the regions. Either people could move to other regions for employment, or, if unemployment were high new investment might move to regions with lower wage costs. According to this approach, regional assistance would merely make it more difficult to achieve economic restructuring because firms would be encouraged to invest in ways which were likely to be inefficient, so that in the long run matters would continue to deteriorate.

The surviving regional policy was a particularly troublesome aspect of the welfare state for the new government. It seemed to run directly counter to an approach which stressed the self-equilibrating strengths of the free market and to present irritating obstacles to necessary economic restructuring. Still worse, in some ways, it channelled financial support to the Labour heartlands in Scotland, Wales and the North of England in ways which merely increased dependence on the state and encouraged regionally based corporatist alliances between business, trade unions and the state. Not surprisingly, the policy was an early target for reform, and by the mid-1980s there was no longer any explicit central government programme seeking to redistribute industry between regions, except on an *ad hoc* basis of encouragement to individual firms, or through competition between development agencies (particularly in Scotland, Wales and Northern Ireland).

It could also be argued that the economic and political justifications for having a regional policy were becoming less pressing. The problems of economic decline and the pressures for large scale restructuring now extended far beyond the 'regions', and affected even the previously prosperous parts of the country. They could no longer be defined as the special problems of particular areas. At the end of the 1970s it was widely accepted that the problems of economic decline and deindustrialization in Britain were not restricted to the traditional regions — the 'distressed areas' of an earlier slump in the 1930s. The United Kingdom as a whole seemed to have been excluded from the growing prosperity of Western Europe. In other words, the issue was not so much about equalizing regional disparities within the UK, but about improving the position of the UK *as a region within Europe*. In terms of the local-global distinction, the UK could be seen as local within the wider global context of Europe, to the extent that a focus on the regions as 'local' within a 'global' context defined as the UK, no longer made economic or political sense. Perhaps, as the new Conservative government suggested, now was the time to move towards more widespread restructuring directed towards national economic and political renewal rather than a continuation of genteel decay.

SUMMARY

- Until the 1970s, regional politics was oriented towards the UK state, because it provided financial assistance and many industries were nationalized.

- The existing basis of regional politics was eroded after the mid 1970s, when national policy began to emphasize that the UK as a whole faced problems of economic decline, and needed to reorientate towards Europe.

- Traditional regional policy was an expression of the social reformist tradition which came under challenge from arguments within the liberal tradition in the late 1970s.

2.3 TOWARDS NEW REGIONAL AND NATIONALIST POLITICS?

Perhaps the end of the old regional arrangements does not have to mean the end of regional politics. If the old model of regional politics was built around a series of linkages through a national state system to a set of international economic structures which have changed fundamentally, maybe those changes could encourage a higher degree of regional autonomy, in the context of a potentially weaker UK state.

At the beginning of the 1990s, however, it has to be admitted that, despite all the changes in the economic position of the English regions, the central UK state was proving reluctant to give up its powers. The context might have changed, but the political response was less clear cut. Indeed, arguably one consequence was an *increased* stress on central power, alongside the run-down of regional policy. Within a market economy it is argued by those in the liberal tradition that the role of the state should be limited: in the case of the UK, up to the early 1990s, that was interpreted to mean opposition to new layers of government, leaving only central government with political legitimacy. In the mid 1980s the metropolitan county councils which might have been seen as possible bases for regional government (including Greater Manchester, Merseyside, Tyne and Wear and the West Midlands) were abolished, along with the Greater London Council. There were limited signs of moves towards regional government, in proposals from Labour and the Liberal Democrats, but it was not possible to identify any substantial regionally based political movements or institutions within England.

Most of the signs of regional activity looked like pale echoes of the old alliances for growth. In general they arose from local government initiatives and were almost always directed towards the achievement of economic growth. The long tradition of joint regional campaigning and development companies in the North of England has been sustained in recent years. A series of attempts has been made to construct regional organizations capable of linking councils, industry and trade unions to speak for the North. The resulting agencies have sometimes been presented as offering a basis for regional government, but more often as providing a platform from which to lobby central government for support and a focus of promotional activity for the region as a whole.

Typical campaigns have included those for regional airports, improved rail connections and demands for a Channel Tunnel terminal to be located in the North of England. And regional initiatives sponsored by local governments have spread more widely. Even in the South East of England, SEEDS (South East Economic Development Strategy) brought together a group of councils concerned, as the name suggests, jointly to develop strategies for the South East and to indicate some of the particular problems and possibilities which existed there, although in this case the problems of 'growth' are also matters of concern so there was a move beyond the old model of growth alliances. In some regions agencies originally set up by local councils to foster economic development — such as local enterprise boards — extended their ambitions to cover wider areas (examples include the West Midlands Enterprise Board and Yorkshire Enterprise).

In principle, however, the break-up of the old economic logic which held the UK's regions together, both internally and as part of the UK system suggests the possibility of developing alternative bases for political action, no longer based on alliances for growth dominated by major economic interests such as large firms and trade unions. There has been a gradual rise of debate over issues which have not in the past been given a high priority. Environmental issues, for example, are often tackled in specifically local or regional terms. It has proved possible to mobilize substantial support over particular proposals for change — for example, over the construction of new motorways, the siting of nuclear waste dumps, the building of rail links to the Channel Tunnel and housing development in the 'green belt'. Territorially based coalitions have been constructed, at local and regional levels, which have sometimes been of sufficient force substantially to restrict the scope for manoeuvre of governments and developers.

Outside England the signs of alternative bases for political behaviour seem to be clearer, and the dissolution of the UK glue seems to be clearer, too. The 1970s saw a substantial rise in support for nationalist politics in Wales and Scotland. The referendum votes on devolution at the end of the decade were officially viewed as inconclusive (with a 'no' vote being recorded in Wales and a 'yes' vote in Scotland, but on a relatively low turn-out) but the pressures for devolution, home rule and even independence have continued since then, with substantial votes for nationalist parties in both countries, particularly Scotland. The argument that the UK is no longer a suitable state through which to develop policy in an increasingly globalized and Europeanized setting has been a major plank in the arguments of the Scottish National Party, which favours the development of an independent Scotland within a more federal European Community, rather than a United Kingdom.

Northern Ireland, too, has been substantially affected by the restructuring which we have been discussing. Since the early 1970s, there has been a break between the political elites of Northern Ireland and those of the UK. Ulster Unionism has fragmented and can no longer be assumed to be a regional (and generally loyal) wing of the Conservative Party as was once the case. And, of course, despite partially successful attempts to build up other parties (such as the Social Democratic and Labour Party) as alternatives for the Catholic community, republicanism has also maintained considerable support throughout this period. The position of Northern Ireland seems increasingly anomalous — part, yet not part, of the UK. Its economy is losing many of its links to the rest of the UK economy, particularly following the privatization of its shipyards, and its politics seem to bear little relationship to decision making in Westminster. Its parties are never likely to find a place in a UK government despite the commitment of the various Unionist parties to the institutions of the UK. The Anglo-Irish agreement of the late 1980s between the UK government and that of the Irish Republic clearly implied that Northern Ireland was not a region like any other, since it allowed the government of another country some influence over policy making. Despite attempts to set up regional branches of UK parties, the main political issue in Northern Ireland remains, precisely, whether the Union should survive and not what the UK government should be doing on a wide range of issues.

It is not easy to draw any final conclusions about the nature and direction of the changes taking place within the UK's regions and component nations. I have highlighted some features which suggest that there is scope for a revived territorial politics at those levels, but have also expressed some scepticism about its significance — in England at least. So, maybe this is a good time to remind ourselves of one of the issues raised in Unit 23: 'On the one hand,' it is suggested, 'internationalization is making the national level less important ... On the other hand, it is argued that the regional level might be becoming less important than the local, particularly as the big mining and manufacturing industries, which dominated whole parts of the country, have gone into decline' (Unit 23, Section 2.2)

How does this relate to political questions? It implies that the regional level may be losing its importance, since there is less holding it together in economic terms. But regional identity is not simply the product of economic forces. Representations of regional and national identity can be very powerful in their own right. And this seems to be particularly important within the UK's nations. Economic change may reduce the importance of the national level in politics, and open up opportunities at regional level and for the UK's component nations. But it may even be — as Unit 17 suggests —that the rise of support for nationalism in Wales and Scotland has taken place at just the time when its economic base is being undermined, when political fragmentation to still smaller territorial units is becoming more possible and more extensive.

So in the next section, I want to consider whether and how the local level may be increasing in importance as a site for political debate.

SUMMARY

- The changed economic position of the UK within the international system has had ambiguous results. There are limited signs of a new regional politics; but also signs of centralization by the UK state.

- There has been a rise of nationalist politics in Wales and Scotland which suggests a growing challenge to the unity of the United Kingdom within a European context.

- The position of Northern Ireland within the UK has also been questioned, and has changed since the late 1960s.

- Internationalization may be making the national and regional levels less important, while the local level increases in significance.

---

3   THE SIGNIFICANCE OF LOCAL POLITICS

This part of the unit seeks to assess the vitality and significance of local politics in the UK with the help of two forms of evidence: the first quantitative and the second rather more qualititative. In Section 3.1, national and local voting figures are examined in ways which should help us to judge the importance of variations between support for political parties in different places. In the sections which follow, the focus shifts towards a consideration of the experience at local level, indicating how different groups may interact in particular localities to generate a distinctive local politics.

3.1   DIFFERENCES IN VOTING BEHAVIOUR

If local politics is to be much more than a local expression of national politics, then we need to be able to identify significant differences between political behaviour in different places. That is not as straightforward as one might expect. Until the early 1980s, the widespread belief, as far as general elections were concerned, was that 'to know the swing in Cornwall was to know, within a percentage or two, the swing in the Highlands' (Crewe 1985, p.103). It was largely taken for granted that one of the reasons for long term political stability in the UK, was that electors tended to vote along lines of occupational class, so that Labour MPs and Labour councils would be elected in places where there were high concentrations of manual workers, whilst Conservative MP's and Conservative councils would be elected in places where there were high concentrations of non-manual, professional and managerial employees. It was assumed that women living with men would vote in accordance with the occupational categorization of those men. Northern Ireland was almost always excluded from consideration for being exceptional and having somehow aberrant voting patterns, no sooner noted than ignored.

Similarly, it was maintained that voting in local elections bore little relationship to local political issues, but was instead largely the product of shifts in national voting preferences. On the basis of his study of Birmingham, using figures from the 1960s which compared voting in Birmingham to those of England as a whole (see Figure 1), it was concluded that local elections, 'are determined overwhelmingly by national political considerations. Local elections are a sort of annual general election' (Newton, 1976, p.16). The pattern of national and local trends shown in Figure 1 suggests that voting moved in roughly the same direction at the same time in Birmingham and England. In other words, there was a strong *correlation* between voting in Birmingham and the rest of England. A high correlation means that they tend to move together. It is important to note that it does not necessarily imply that one leads to — or is the cause of — the other. In this case, however, it would suggest that there was little special or exceptional about Birmingham which might have encouraged substantially different forms of voting behaviour at local level. Not only did the overall voting figures seem to suggest a remarkable degree of uniformity, at least until the 1970s, but the rather low level of turn-out in local elections (30-40 per cent, when in general elections it was around 70-80 per cent) also seemed to confirm that local politics was not very dynamic. It appeared that most voters agreed that it was national decisions which mattered, even for those activities nominally administered at local level.

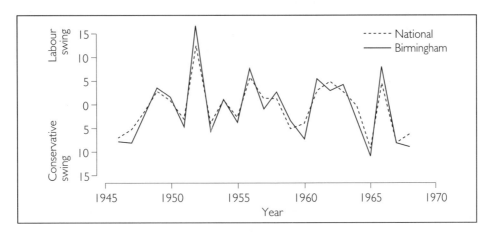

Figure 1   Birmingham and the national swing

More recently, however, some of these assumptions have begun to come under challenge. In broad terms, apparent differences between electoral behaviour are not difficult to find, as George Jones and John Stewart noted in a survey of the local elections in 1982:

> In Wolverhampton, Labour made gains while in nearby Walsall Labour lost seats. Whereas in Bradford and Leeds Labour lost ground, in Barnsley they made large gains and in Sheffield they maintained their position. In Rochdale, Labour lost seats, while in Oldham Labour gained seats. In Strathclyde Labour made gains, but not in Lothian.
>
> (Jones and Stewart, 1983, p.17)

In 1990, too, when Labour's share of the vote increased dramatically across most of England and Wales, the Conservatives were still able to hold on to and win additional seats in Wandsworth and Westminster and to gain Ealing, while Labour's share of the vote also fell slightly in Scotland. The only possible explanation for such variation, according to Jones and Stewart lies in the identification of specifically local factors, debates and disagreements over local issues and choices made at local level. In 1990, for example, it has been argued that levels of community charge or poll tax may have influenced voting behaviour in some places.

There are increasing signs of variation in local elections. Swings of support between parties can no longer confidently be asserted to be nationally uniform. In UK-wide elections, too, the importance of geographical variation in voting behaviour is increasingly widely acknowledged. I shall use figures from the 1987 general election to provide some evidence of this. In the initial press analyses of the election it was frequently noted that Labour was by far the leading party in Scotland, with the Conservatives substantially losing support, and modest but significant support for the Scottish National Party. Although Labour remained dominant in Wales, its recovery since 1979 was little better than the UK average. In England the Conservatives had consolidated their position in the South, with Labour remaining strong in the North. There was, it was concluded, a North-South divide in political as well as economic terms, as well as a widening division between rural and urban areas, particularly the inner cities. The structure of parties and voting in Northern Ireland remained sharply different from that in the rest of the UK, with none of the main UK parties being directly represented.

Table 1   The Percentage of the electorate voting for the Conservative, Labour and Alliance (Liberal in 1979) Parties, 1979-1987, by geographical region.

		Conservative			Labour			Alliance		
		1979	1983	1987	1979	1983	1987	1979	1983	1987
1	Strathclyde	19.5	16.2	13.8	35.0	31.1	41.6	3.9	15.1	11.1
2	East. Scotland	20.8	19.9	19.0	30.2	25.7	33.6	6.1	18.0	14.7
3	Rural Scotland	22.7	22.4	22.1	14.7	10.7	15.9	10.7	18.8	19.8
4	Rural North	35.0	34.8	35.2	25.7	18.6	22.3	13.1	19.3	18.4
5	Industrial Northeast	24.4	22.1	20.9	39.5	30.9	38.2	7.9	17.5	15.1
6	Merseyside	29.7	24.7	21.2	33.1	28.6	36.2	9.7	16.5	17.2
7	Greater Manchester	30.9	26.9	27.8	33.8	27.4	32.0	10.2	17.0	15.2
8	Rest of Northwest	35.7	33.2	33.6	29.4	23.8	28.7	9.8	17.2	15.1
9	West Yorks	27.9	26.4	28.3	33.9	25.7	31.3	10.7	18.5	15.7
10	South Yorks	21.8	19.1	17.7	41.3	33.4	41.2	7.9	15.8	13.3
11	Rural Wales	26.1	26.0	26.7	24.6	17.8	23.9	11.5	17.6	17.4
12	Industrial South Wales	22.7	20.1	20.8	40.8	32.3	42.5	6.3	16.4	12.2
13	West Midlands Conurbation	32.4	29.0	30.4	32.8	26.6	29.5	5.6	14.3	12.4
14	Rest of West Midlands	35.8	36.1	37.3	25.7	18.3	20.6	11.6	19.9	19.1
15	East Midlands	35.0	34.7	37.5	28.8	20.8	23.5	10.1	17.7	16.1
16	East Anglia	37.5	37.9	40.0	24.3	15.5	17.0	11.8	21.1	19.8
17	Devon and Cornwall	40.1	39.3	38.2	14.8	8.0	12.3	19.8	28.2	26.2
18	Wessex	38.3	38.2	40.0	20.1	12.4	13.5	15.3	23.2	24.1
19	Inner London	25.5	21.7	24.2	31.7	27.3	27.5	6.3	14.1	14.0
20	Outer London	37.5	34.3	38.0	26.1	17.2	18.8	10.0	18.3	16.0
21	Outer Metropolitan	40.3	39.9	42.7	20.6	12.2	13.3	12.5	21.0	19.8
22	Outer Southeast	40.4	40.0	41.8	18.9	11.1	12.4	13.1	21.2	21.5
National		32.3	30.7	31.8	27.7	20.5	24.6	10.2	18.5	17.1

Source: Johnston, R. J., Pattie, C. J., and Allsop, J. C., *A Nation Dividing? The Electoral Map of Great Britain, 1979–1987*, Longman (1988).

Figure 2   The geography of seats won, 1987.

Source: Johnston, R. J., Pattie, C. J., and Allsop, J. C., *A Nation Dividing? The Electoral Map of Great Britain, 1979–1987*, Longman (1988).

———————————————— ACTIVITY 3 ————————————————

Figure 2 shows the broad pattern of voting in 1987, with a stark division across the face of a computerized Great Britain, in which each square represents a constituency. But the process of change is shown in more detail by the information given in Table 1, which indicates the changing levels of support for different parties in different places over the three elections of 1979, 1983, and 1987. You should note that these are percentages of the electorate and not of those voting, so that proportions may be lower than you are accustomed to seeing in the press. Remember that this information only covers Great Britain — Northern Ireland is excluded — and that support for nationalist and other parties is not recorded. The Alliance was made up of the Liberal Party (now Liberal Democratic Party) and the now defunct Social Democratic Party, which put together joint manifestos in 1983 and 1987.

Table 1 shows the overall figures for voting share, and you may wish to note what happened in the region in which you live (if you are not sure which that is, check with the map in Figure 3). In addition, look down the different columns and try to identify some of the major shifts in share across the three elections. Were they the same everywhere, either in direction or magnitude? To start, look particularly at Strathclyde, Merseyside, Inner and Outer London.

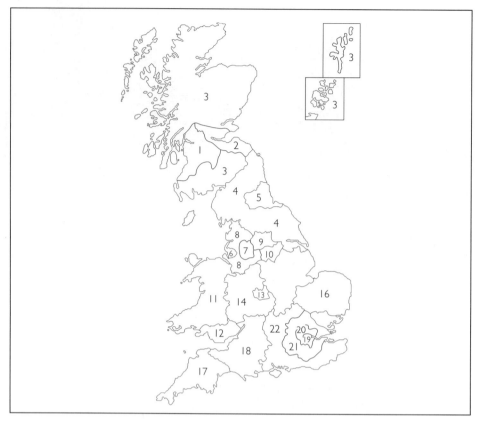

Figure 3   The twenty-two geographical regions

Source: Johnston, R. J., Pattie, C. J., and Allsop, J. C., *A Nation Dividing? The Electoral Map of Great Britain, 1979–1987*, Longman (1988).

Some changes are quite dramatic. In Strathclyde, for example, the Conservative vote was down to less than 14 per cent of the electorate in 1987, having fallen consistently over the years since 1979. Labour's vote was below 14 per cent in four areas (Devon and Cornwall, Wessex, Outer Metropolitan and Outer South East England). In all areas the Alliance vote had risen significantly since 1979, but had been patchy since 1983, up slightly in some regions, down slightly in others. Conservative support fell sharply in Scotland, particularly Strathclyde, Industrial North East England, Merseyside (dramatically), Greater Manchester and South Yorkshire. Labour support fell sharply over the 1979–87 period in Rural North England, the West Midlands Conurbation, the Rest of the West Midlands, the East Midlands, East Anglia, Wessex, Inner London, Outer London, the Outer Metropolitan area, and Outer South East England. In the Southern regions of England, the Conservative vote generally increased between 1983 and 1987, while Labour's fell; in the Northern and urban regions of England, Scotland, and Wales Labour's rose and the Conservatives' fell. The rise of the Alliance vote throughout Great Britain limited the overall scope for Labour's vote to rise.

These figures only cover one decade, and the precise pattern of voting behaviour is likely to change over time, particularly as support for third (fourth or fifth) parties rises and falls. But the overall pattern of differentiation within Great Britain is clear enough and it looks as if the divisions are becoming more marked. Acknowledging the extent of support for nationalist parties in Scotland and Wales and the range of unionist parties in Northern Ireland, would tend to reinforce this conclusion. It is less clear what the explanations for these patterns of differentiation might be. In this case, the pattern of uneven development can be identified relatively easily, but exploring the processes which underlie it is rather more difficult.

SUMMARY

- Some people argue that local political behaviour is largely an expression of national politics with little geographical variation.
- More recent evidence suggests that there is substantial variation which cannot easily be explained in terms of national swings.

3.2   FROM DIFFERENCE TO POLITICS

Having identified differences we need to explain why they arise and how they are sustained. Reference back to the discussions of uneven development in the earlier units of the block is helpful here, because they stress the ways in which layers of development build up, each previous layer influencing the next, in such a way that each place becomes unique, yet is also influenced by wider processes of economic development. The notion of layers of development is not one which has to be restricted to discussions of the economy. On the contrary, whilst a focus on the economy is a useful starting point, because it makes it possible to show the model in a relatively simplified form, any developed analysis of uneven development needs to include some consideration of the ways in which the economy relates to other aspects of our social existence. How a local economy develops will itself be influenced by local social relations and local political relations (as well as by their interaction with national and international levels). And, of course, local social structures and political practice will also be influenced by the nature of the local economy and its history. Past development has consequences for the present which need to be explored, as it interacts with global processes of economic and political restructuring.

It is useful to remind ourselves here of some of the points made in Section 2 of Unit 23. Localities are the products of interaction between people, groups and institutions in particular places over time. And this interaction is influenced by legacies (even memories and representations) from the past which have helped produce those places. What matters is the processes which take place within a locality and their interaction with a wider (global) system, rather than any narrowly defined institutional framework or boundary imposed by a Parliamentary Boundary Commissioner or a local council. Since localities are socially constructed, it is difficult to define them from above. As the discussion of Hackney in Unit 23 shows, there may even be conflict between groups over how to define them. So, for our purposes, one of the key messages to be drawn from Unit 23, is that interaction between groups and activities may generate locally specific forms of political behaviour, which cannot simply be deduced from overall national figures or political trends.

──────────────────── ACTIVITY 4 ────────────────────

How would you define your own local area?

This may seem a peculiar question to ask. We normally just take our local environment for granted and, in fact, we probably all live in a series of overlapping local areas: different areas in which we feel 'at home' for different purposes. So, it may be helpful to start off by thinking about how you would label or name your local area to someone asking where you lived, before going on to consider how this relates to your other interpretations of that area, e.g. for shopping, work, study, friendship etc.

My guess is that your definition will vary for different purposes. So that it is quite easy for you to view yourself as part of an immediate geographical area — perhaps where you do local shopping, or visit friends by foot, perhaps it includes local schools, or a doctor's surgery — but also to place yourself within a wider context — for weekly or specialist shopping, say, or your study centre, or local college — and you may be able to identify with a wider area still — the conurbation, sub region, town or city within which you live, or the area within which you travel to work. Some people who live quite close to each other may have quite different views of the places within which they both appear to live. There are likely to be differences depending on race, class, gender and age. And on where you live — town, village, hamlet, inner city or suburb. Estate agents might have quite different definitions too. Perhaps you could think of some of the reasons for all these differences.

—————————————————— ACTIVITY 5 ——————————————————

Finally, what would you identify as the main influences on your own political behaviour? That may not be something you've thought about before, so it might be helpful just to jot down those elements of your life which you think influence your own thinking. For example: friends, family, workplace, community groups, local and national newspapers, political parties, council etc. Try to categorize each as local or national, since the interaction between these levels is crucial in shaping your local political environment.

Influence	Local	National

I suggest that you add your notes and conclusions to Activities 4 and 5 to your Resource File if you are keeping one, since they may be helpful in preparing for TMA06.

———

A focus on local political environments does not imply a more or less unchanging local political culture which *determines* the behaviour of those who experience it. On the contrary, there is a constant interaction between social classes, groups, political parties, individuals, national and local government, local and global processes. This shapes and reshapes the nature of the local political environment and it is important to identify and explore the processes of interaction which generate different political patterns and practices in different places. Not only is it here that, as Johnston puts it, people learn 'the political meanings of their class positions' (Johnston, *et al* 1988, p.269), but it is in this context that classes and other groups define themselves through their own activity, rather than being created from above in the rather dry categories of the statistician.

The importance of this is confirmed in a detailed study of the 1987 general election, some of whose findings we have already considered in Activity 3. Its authors concluded that people in all class categories were likely to identify with the party closest to the 'dominant local ideology' in their area. Here 'ideology' is being used to describe a package of attitudes to politics, economy, welfare, family and social life, particularly as reflected in identification with one or other of the main political parties. According to the authors of the study, the 'dominant local ideology' tended to be a function of an area's occupational class composition, so that in those which had high concentrations of manual workers and the unemployed it would tend to favour Labour. Where the ideology closest to Labour was dominant, a higher proportion of all classes was more likely to be sympathetic to Labour (although not necessarily Labour voters) than in an area where the 'dominant local ideology' was closest to that of the Conservatives. So even among occupational classes whose members would 'normally' be expected to support the Conservatives, a higher proportion would be sympathetic to Labour in the former areas. In the 1987 election, some areas — such as the coalfields — supported Labour to an even greater extent than might have been expected from their occupational structure, whilst others (particularly in parts of the South East) did so to a lesser extent (Johnston, Pattie and Allsopp 1988, p.269).

The researchers suggest that this reinforcement of support for the locally dominant political party, can only be explained in terms of locality effects. Local and regional identification becomes a significant element in the formation of classes and social groups, to the extent that a local or regional consciousness may be developed. This is also stressed by Beynon *et al* in Chapter 21 of the Course Reader in their discussion of Teesside, where they outline some of the ways in which such a consciousness might develop over time. Other forms of consciousness which find particular local expressions may also be important. At least until 1987, levels of support for the Labour party were much higher in constituencies which included significant Afro-Caribbean communities than in those with otherwise similar class compositions. And similar — if not quite so marked — differences could be identified for constituencies with large Asian communities. One explanation for this pattern of voting may be that support for Labour is reinforced by the degree of concentration of such communities within relatively small areas in Britain's cities.

SUMMARY

- The notions of uneven development and layers of development are useful in understanding the significance of local political differences.
- Politics is learned through processes of interaction within local political environments.
- Local and regional consciousness may play a significant part in the ways in which individuals develop their position within classes.

3.3   LOCAL POLITICS IN PRACTICE

Politics is not just about voting. It is about a whole range of activities intended to influence (and sometimes replace) the state. What expression does this have at local level?

DIFFERENCES BETWEEN COUNCILS

In most discussions of local politics, whatever their theoretical starting point, the main focus of attention tends to be placed on the operation of local councils and activity related to them, for example through lobbying and campaigns. Although there are good reasons for questioning this starting point (for example, because it seems to exclude other forms of collective self-activity from consideration), it is a helpful way into discussion. All of us can probably identify our local councils, and many of us will have had direct contact with them — at least through the payment of local taxes, the experience of housing, schooling, social services or planning policies. Many people are employed directly or indirectly by local councils. As a result councils have the highest profile of any locally based political institution and much local political activity does, of necessity, end up being oriented towards them as sources of funds and agencies of control.

There is a substantial variation in the organization of local government across different parts of the UK. In England and Wales, much of the country is organized into county councils (responsible for such activities as primary and secondary education and social services) and district councils (responsible for activities such as housing, development, control, domestic refuse disposal). But in most large conurbations (including Leeds, Sheffield, Manchester and Birmingham but with notable exceptions such as Bristol, Cardiff, Nottingham, Southampton and Swansea) metropolitan district councils are responsible for all those main activities and there are no county councils. In London, since the abolition of the Greater London Council and Inner London Educational Authority, the borough councils have substantially the same responsibilities as the metropolitan districts. Scotland is organized on a different basis with regional, island and district councils. Regional councils are responsible for activities such as social services and strategic planning, district councils for most other activities, and in areas with island councils, there are no districts and all local authority activities are undertaken by the island councils. In Northern Ireland, there are only district councils, which have very limited responsibilities and budgets, largely restricted to street cleaning, managing cemeteries and leisure centres. Housing and social services are the responsibility of other (non-elected) agencies.

Levels of expenditure vary significantly between local authorities. According to figures collected and tabulated by the Chartered Institute of Public Finance and Accountancy (CIFPA) (which is the organization of the accounting profession in much of the public sector in England and Wales), differences in expenditure per head vary significantly between authorities. Figure 4 shows the extent of variation from the average expenditure for local authorities on a regional basis.

Even within London, when the Audit Commission compared spending between similar authorities on a range of activities it found, perhaps unsurprisingly, that some Conservative controlled councils (including Wandsworth and Westminster) spent substantially less than some Labour councils, with similar problems (e.g. on housing and cleansing). But the Commission also identified substantial differences between Labour councils (Audit Commission 1987).

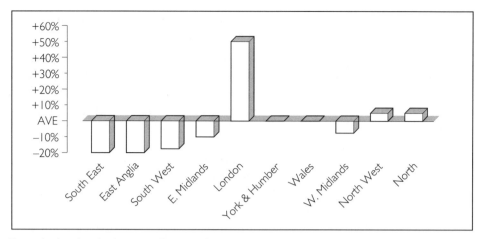

Figure 4   Local authority expenditure per head, by region (England and Wales)

So how can these differences be explained? They are so large that it is unlikely that they can be satisfactorily explained solely in terms of either party political control or of some 'objective' assessment of local 'need'. In its report on the London authorities, the Audit Commission went on to argue for bringing spending levels closer together, in order to achieve comparable 'effectiveness' at high levels of 'efficiency'. In other words, they tended to explain the differences simply in terms of the greater (or lesser) efficiency of different councils. But it is reasonable to conclude that at least some of the difference may be explicable in terms of differing political priorities even between councils nominally controlled by the same party.

It was probably always the case that differences between councils could not be explained solely in terms of differences between political parties, but this became particularly apparent in the 1980s. The most obvious area of differentiation was between Labour authorities. Some councils, including the Greater London Council, Sheffield, Walsall, Stirling, and several London Boroughs among others, were identified as part of a trend towards 'local socialism', and a break with the old traditions of 'municipal labourism' with which many other Labour councils were still associated. Similar distinctions were made between Conservative controlled councils, as some, such as Dudley, Wandsworth, Westminster and, for a short time, Bradford, were identified as 'flagships' for Thatcherism in their commitment to privatization, whilst others remained more traditional and reliant on the advice of professional officers. Once this is accepted, then a different world of local politics begins to open up — one in which it becomes important to look more closely at the development of interaction between groups and interests at local level, as well as the interaction between local political activity and politics at the national (and possibly international) levels.

PRESSURE GROUPS AND SOCIAL MOVEMENTS

This seems to be confirmed by other research. In his report to the Widdicombe Committee, for example, John Gyford confirmed that there was a trend towards wider consultation by local authorities of a range of sectional interests, including those representing ethnic minorities and voluntary organizations. The move towards increased consultation can, he suggests, 'be seen as a direct reflection of social trends which are leading away from a rather quiescent and largely homogeneous mass society towards one that is both more assertive and more diversified' involving 'a proliferation of pressure groups at both local and national level, devoted to the achievement of quite particularized goals in such areas as pollution and the environment, sexual behaviour, media policy, animal welfare, homelessness, transport policy, energy policy and disarmament and defence' (Gyford, 1986 p.109).

There has been a growth of locally based political campaigns and activities through the 1980s and into the 1990s. Often these have been 'community' based, including tenants' campaigns over rent levels or repairs, or crime prevention. Or they have been amenity based, in defence of green spaces, or against new road schemes, or even in favour of constructing a park. Local politics has also become an important focus for debate on issues of race and gender, as women's groups and black organizations have organized at local level to campaign on a range of issues, from policing to education and equal opportunities. Frequently these campaigns have been directed towards local councils, whether because the council is directly involved as planning authority, provider or landlord or because it is seen as a potential source of financial or political support. But sometimes they imply self-help alternatives to state provision, for example, in attempting to set up housing cooperatives, or networks of hostels for Women's Aid, in developing local campaigns about racially based attacks on young people, or in seeking to generate a viable local infrastructure of anti-racist campaigning. In Northern Ireland single purpose community organizations are sometimes set up to avoid the conflicts generated by the official politics focused around the question of the union with the UK. Solomos notes the importance of community based organizations within Afro-Caribbean and Asian communities, in placing new items on the policy agenda, particularly on education, relations with the police, black unemployment and racial attacks (Solomos, 1989, pp.148–9). The local politics of gender and 'race' have become important means of defining the position of previously excluded groups within the British political and social system.

Locally based politics are as likely to involve the organizing of concerts as much as demonstrations, the recycling of paper and cans as much as putting up candidates for election. Paul Gilroy argues that mass movements may develop at local level around the politics of 'race' in ways which cut across traditional divisions between the public and the private spheres, as new institutions are created: 'temples, churches, clubs, cafes and blues dances, confound any eurocentric idea of where the line dividing politics and culture should fall' (Gilroy, 1987, p.37).

NEW INITIATIVES

Meanwhile, there have also been important developments within the official structures of local government. There has, for example, been a growing confidence among councils of otherwise quite different political stripes that it is possible to develop independent policies intended to reflect the needs of their localities and regions. This has been particularly clear in the field of economic development to which brief reference has already been made. A great deal of research confirms that there was a major expansion of local economic development work throughout the 1980s (e.g. Mills and Young, 1986). By the middle of the decade, councils were already spending significantly more on economic activities than was being spent on regional policy by central government, even on the basis of relatively conservative estimates of local expenditure. This development took place without councils having any formal responsibility in the area, at least until the passing of the Local Government and Housing Act 1989 which gave them explicit powers but restricted how much they could spend and how it could be spent.

The expansion of economic development work is of interest for other reasons, too, because it also seems to have encouraged the development of another series of linkages which have begun to bypass the central government of the UK. Several councils have their own links with businesses in countries such as

Japan, the USA, and the Federal Republic of Germany, and have even made visits to the USSR or China, with a view to attracting trade and investment. Some, such as Strathclyde, have their own offices in Brussels in order to take advantage of assistance from the European regional and social funds.

We shall consider some of the implications of these interactions in the next section which focuses on the increasing significance of Europe, but it confirms a vitality of policy development at local level, as well as the importance of local politics in shaping political attitudes which we have already noted. So, whatever we conclude about the position of the regions, it looks as if localities are developing as focuses for political activity, even if central government retains important powers of control and the value of local autonomy has not been formally recognized. Although one consequence of increased local activity in the 1980s seems to have been the imposition of tighter financial controls and the abolition of some particularly troublesome councils (the metropolitan counties and the Greater London Council), control has proved difficult to achieve and initiatives continue to develop at local level.

=============================== READER ===============================

Read the sections headed 'Economic expansion of the role of local policy' in Chapter 20 of the Course Reader (pp.212-15). These outline Swindon's positive involvement in economic development activity. Try to identify the main forces behind Swindon's expansion. In particular, consider:

- the role of central government
- the role of local government
- the role of local political parties.

Has the significance of these changed over time?

The conclusions I would draw from the Swindon experience are fairly straight-forward. First, the role of central government between the early 1950s and mid 1980s was largely supportive. The expansion of Swindon was encouraged both positively (particularly through its approval as a town development scheme), and as a consequence of other state policies (such as the expansion of Heathrow Airport and the building of the M4). But later the emphasis on expansion resulted in Thamesdown (the district council within which Swindon is located) being penalized by the central government's imposition of financial controls in the mid 1980s. Second, local government played a key part at the core of a pro-growth coalition from the 1950s onwards, bringing together political parties, unions, existing employers and developers. From the mid 1980s again, the centrality of its role has been reduced a little because it has little land left for development and the emphasis has shifted to advocacy and marketing. There is some evidence that private developers have had to take on the initiative, preparing proposals for new development, which have been approved by central government. Third, there is also evidence that the old pro-growth coalition has lost is strength. Interests are now being reflected within local political parties (particularly Labour), which suggest that it may now be appropriate to restrict growth and defend local amenities. Economic policies remain a significant issue within local politics, but at the start of the 1990s, they were more contentious than they had been in the past.

SUMMARY

- There are substantial differences in spending levels between similar councils.
- These cannot easily be explained in terms of party political differences or objective criteria of 'need'.
- There are significant differences in political behaviour between councils controlled by the same party.
- Important aspects of local politics exist outside the council, in particular:

  — non-elected governments

  — community based organizations (e.g. organized on issues of gender and race).

- There has been a growth of non-traditional activity (particularly economic development) by many local authorities which brings them into direct contact with Europe.

4   DEVELOPING A EUROPEAN DIMENSION

There seems to be some evidence that localities and their politics are becoming more important, even if that evidence is by no means conclusive. What evidence is there that the national level is becoming less important, possibly being replaced by the international, in politics as well as economics? In this section of the unit I shall be looking at that question, with the help of a particular focus on the European level. First, I shall look at the European Community, before moving on to a consideration of a more widely defined Europe. The institutions of the European Community and some of the issues raised by its growth have already been introduced in Unit 14 and in TV07. Those materials concentrated specifically on sovereignty and the ways in which UK sovereignty might be under threat from the creation of new supranational institutions. Here we want to explore rather different, although related questions. Whatever the formal constitutional position, we want to consider whether and how relations are changing; the extent to which, and ways in which, relations are developing in practice which are beginning to supersede old arrangements; and the extent to which new arrangements are becoming possible. Are we moving towards a Europe in which regional and local divisions are of more importance than national divisions, and, if so, is this finding any institutional expression? These issues are also explored in TV13, with the help of case studies of two localities, one in the UK (Sheffield in South Yorkshire) and one in France (Lille in Nord-Pas de Calais).

4.1   FROM ECONOMIC TO POLITICAL UNITY?

There are two dominant approaches to the analysis of the European Community: the first stresses its economic aspects and the second its political possibilities. Running alongside these it is possible to identify a marxist critique which tries to bring together the economic and political aspects.

LIBERAL MARKET APPROACHES

The first of these approaches couches its arguments in terms of liberal capitalism and neo-classical economics. It argues for the creation of a free market throughout Europe, sometimes behind a protective tariff and sometimes as a first step towards the wider international liberalization of trade. The justification for such a policy is usually presented in terms of competition between Europe and the United States of America and, more recently, Japan, and the need to build a more competitive European economy. Within the Community, it is hoped that the creation of such a market will encourage substantial restructuring, involving the creation of major trans-European companies, constructed through mergers between existing nationally based enterprises. The EC is supported as a means of removing obstacles to trade and hidden subsidies. A single market is expected to reward the efficient and penalize the inefficient.

The founding treaty (The Treaty of Rome, 1957) included provision for European institutions (such as a Social Fund and an Investment Bank) but the European Community's key features appeared to be economic rather than political, expressed in the term 'common market' which it was usually given in the UK at the time. At the end of the treaty were to be found page after page listing a range of tariffs designed to exclude external competition, whilst the main text expressed a commitment to free competition within the Community. The Single European Act, implemented at the end of 1992 and approved by the parliaments of all the member states, similarly stresses the openness of markets within Europe, moving further towards a unified European economy. One of the most senior European Commissioners has responsibility for competition policy, seeking to ensure that European companies compete with each other on equal terms.

Even the operation of the so-called 'structural funds', such as the regional development fund (ERDF), which provides support for spending on infrastructure in the European Community's most disadvantaged regions, and the social fund (ESF), which provides support for training for the unemployed, can be seen as helping to make the liberal market work more effectively. Such intervention is justified because, 'improving physical communications integrates the market, while training enables adaptation to market-induced changes' (Cutler *et al*, 1989, p.148).

But from this 'liberal' perspective, the role of the European institutions should be severely limited. Their task is to police competition policy to ensure that barriers to trade and travel are reduced and to support the liberal market. One 'liberal' critique of the European Community is that it has taken on a much wider role than is required by its basic functions, and, as Enoch Powell argues forcibly in TV07, may be usurping the sovereignty of its member states. Lewis, too, is scathing about attempts to introduce what he calls 'Eurosocialism', which he claims is supported by the senior officials of the European Community because 'it promises them a vast regulatory empire to rule' (Lewis, 1989, p.6). He believes, that it is possible and necessary to separate the economic and political aspects of the community, so that the market can be defended and the growth of European political institutions effectively resisted.

Others go further to argue that the potential of a single European market (enshrined in the proposals for 1992) is such that it can fatally undermine the power of national and European state bureaucracies. For them 1992 is a 'fantastic dream, a pure exercise in deregulation, the devolution of power to the market and economic federalism ... It says: give a maximum of say to markets, a minimum to Brussels and it will even get national governments off our backs — it even tames Leviathan' (Price, 1988, p.41). Price argues that the task for sympathetic politicians is to fight for this dream, oppose interventionalist tendencies and leave moves towards European federalism 'for future generations to worry about' (Price, 1988, p.42).

INSTITUTIONAL APPROACHES

Although it is in its economic aspects that the European Community has made most progress, it has also been strongly argued that it would be a mistake to see the Community solely as an economic arrangement. According to this perspective, which I have labelled institutional, the origins and development of the European Community have always powerfully combined political and economic elements. In the immediate post-war period moves towards European unity, federation or cooperation were seen to offer a means of reducing the possibility of major conflict between Germany and France, and of providing an alternative to pressures which might encourage such conflict. Politically, too, in a context of domination by major superpowers such as the USA and the USSR, Europe seemed to offer the only possibility of operating on a similar scale. With the partial exception of the UK, which still had a residual belief in its imperial mission and in its 'special arrangement' or partnership with the USA, the political leaders of most European countries began to accept that only collaboration within Europe would give them status on the world political stage. And even in the UK the idea of Europe was at least seen as one option. In 1948 Churchill — often presented as a representative of the 'bulldog breed' — was quite lyrical about the prospects:

> We must proclaim the mission and the design of a United Europe whose moral conception will win the respect and the gratitude of mankind and whose physical strength will be such that none will dare molest her tranquil sway ... I hope to see a Europe where men and women of every country will think as much of being European as of belonging to their native land and wherever they go in this wide domain will truly feel 'Here I am at home'.
>
> (quoted in Sampson, 1971, p.27).

The arguments about creating a European consciousness reflected a view among leading politicians in the countries of Western Europe that new international political and economic rearrangements had made it impossible for Europe's nations (which can be seen as the 'local' level for the purposes of this argument) to continue to operate in the old ways, as completely independent, separate and competing agencies. They needed to find some framework within which they could work together. And perhaps even move towards a united Europe as an alternative focus of political and economic power.

The nature of the united Europe which it was hoped would arise from the ashes of war, was unclear. In its most lyrical form, it seemed to stretch from the 'Atlantic to the Urals'. For others it was explicitly Western European — a barrier against communism. But the dominant set of arguments implied a more pragmatic approach building from economic alliances to political strength. The creation of European economic institutions would, it was hoped, begin to generate a European identity and a European politics. Contrary to the views of Lewis and Price outlined above, it was believed that if Europe united economically, it was also likely to unite politically.

Marquand outlines this vision as follows:

> Economic integration would lead sooner or later to political integration, by solving the practical problems of 'low politics' in the mundane areas affected by the creation of a customs union, the process of integration would gradually 'spill over' into the glamorous areas of foreign, defence and monetary policy, which were the stuff of 'high politics'. Little by little, an irresistible momentum would be set up, which would sweep away the obstacles to full scale political union. The Commission would

evolve into the executive of this union. The Council of Ministers would become the 'upper house' of its legislative, and the directly elected European Parliament the 'lower house'.

(Marquand, 1989, p.209).

In some ways, as Galtung notes, this approach to the development of a European Community has echoes of a marxist position since it assumes that economic organization is basic and changed political forms will flow from it. He quotes an early report of the Community which stated that 'Economic and monetary union thus appears as leaven for the development of political union, which in the long run it (the Community) cannot do without' (Galtung, 1973, p.19). But, of course, its supporters were by no means marxists. On the contrary their policies were being developed partly as an alternative to a perceived threat from communism in the East, and they were committed to the survival and expansion of capitalism in Europe. Their view of politics can best be described as institutionalist, because it was based on negotiation between sovereign states and the gradual construction of new European institutions alongside those states, slowly but inexorably taking over some of their functions and responsibilities.

MARXIST APPROACHES

One marxist interpretation of European developments takes matters rather further. Mandel emphasizes the likelihood of a substantial growth in the development of 'international monopolies', and in particular the growth of European based multinational companies which increasingly have no identifiable national home. On the basis of such a development he suggests there could be a move towards a genuinely federal, supranational state power within Europe. According to Mandel, if the process of economic 'globalization' means the international centralization of capital within Europe, then the existing nationally based state structures will also be under threat. Just as no single nationally based capital will be able to dominate within such a system, so no individual state will be able to dominate and instead there will be a move towards a 'supranational federal state characterized by the transfer of crucial sovereign rights' (Mandel, 1978, p.327).

The evidence for economic shifts along the lines posited by Mandel, however, are still limited or, at least, ambiguous. Since the 1960s, there have been important mergers within Europe, but these have largely taken the form of takeovers initiated by one set of nationally based companies of another — Lucas, for example, has become dominant in motor components manufacture, with plants throughout Europe. At the start of the 1990s there were still not very many 'European' corporations. Most retained identifiable bases in one country or another, and attempts to put together major European consortia have rarely been successful in practice.

The larger European market did help to encourage a wider focus for some firms. In the retail trade, for example, there were signs of firms crossing previously unquestioned national boundaries — in the 1980s Benneton's use of computer systems allowed the company to sustain centralized planning of production, whilst ensuring that the stock of individual shops would be varied according to local demand, and the familiar architectural style of Marks and Spencer was to be found in cities throughout the European Community. Many of the corporations which have most effectively used the unified European market have, however, probably been non-EC based. Firms such as Ford and IBM plan and integrate production across the nations of the European Community, with plants in several of them. And Japanese concerns, such as Komatsu and Nissan (whose development of a plant in Sunderland is discussed in TV12), are able to view it as one market for the output of their local plants, because they do not start from any specific national market base.

So, within Mandel's model, one would expect the political changes associated with modest economic change to be equally modest, particularly if they require the development of specifically European capital. Even if trans-European economic organization is growing, one would not expect that to lead to new forms of supranational state organization, if most firms are still nationally based or the leading transnational companies are non-EC multinationals.

SUMMARY

- Liberal approaches to the European Community stress its role as a common market with free trade internally (and protection externally) to strengthen Europe against America. They suggest it is possible completely to separate economic and political processes.

- Institutional approaches emphasize that economic integration is only a first step in political integration. Indeed, they suggest that one will lead to the other.

- Marxist approaches suggest that increasing internationalization of capital within Europe is likely to lead to a more integrated, federal Europe.

4.2   ASSESSING THE EVIDENCE

A SUPRANATIONAL EUROPE?

When Britain joined the European Community in 1973, the government accepted that some European laws would take precedence over decisions taken within Britain, by the UK Parliament. In other words, courts could enforce decisions on the government, whatever the views of Parliament, if those decisions were in line with European legislation. In principle, such legislation has to be agreed by member states, for example through the Council of Ministers (which is made up of responsible politicians from those states), but not only has the absolute power of veto by individual states been removed since the passing of the Single European Act in 1986, but also once the basic framework of legislation has been agreed, its interpretation may be just as significant, reducing future scope for manoeuvre for governments and politicians.

In other words, the European Community has legal authority over its member states. It is this which leads Dearlove and Saunders to conclude that it is a *supranational* rather than merely an *intergovernmental* agency. Intergovernmental agencies are those — such as the United Nations, the Commonwealth, and the North Atlantic Treaty Organization — which may involve compromise and cooperation between states but 'have no formal authority over the British state ... The British Government is not legally bound to agree to a policy that it does not accept'. Supranational organizations — such as the European Community — are different because they do have legal authority over member states and limit the ability of their parliaments to determine national legislation in some areas (Dearlove and Saunders, 1984, p.419).

Unit 14 shows some of the ways in which membership of the European Community limits UK sovereignty. It is for this reason that it has sometimes been criticized from both right and left: by limiting what member states are able to do, it makes it difficult for parties of the left to introduce industrial policies, involving subsidy and national protectionism, and for parties of the right to cut back on some forms of social legislation which are supported at European level to ensure that some countries do not seek to compete on the basis of reducing social support.

More symbolically, the European Community has also become a forum from which statements are made on a range of wider issues — such as terrorism — on which a European view is felt to be appropriate. In 1990 it was one of the forums used to express a joint European response to Iraq's invasion of Kuwait. Individual states frequently use it to seek support on issues which concern them. Maybe none of this goes as far as the supporters of European unity would want, nor as far as some predicting (and fearing) the rise of a European super state would suggest, but it certainly substantially changes the context of UK politics. And it suggests an independent role for politics which cannot be explained by referring back to the underlying economic organization. The UK has become part of a wider community of more or less equal states, with a set of shared interests, which go beyond military or economic alliances.

It is, of course, important not to exaggerate the significance of all these moves. Even the creation of a (qualified) single market took until 1992 to introduce, and political institutions have been still more slow to develop. Although, directly elected since 1979, the European Parliament still had severely limited powers in the early 1990s. It was able to scrutinize the activities of the European Commission, and even hold up budgetary proposals, but it had negligible powers of implementation. The European Commission (the civil service of the EC) had powers to shape policy and to issue directives, within broad guidelines agreed by the Council of Ministers, but it was the Council of Ministers, and the individual sovereign states which determined the direction of change on most important matters. Although member states were no longer able to use their veto on all issues, change still proceeded at the pace of the slowest moving of the member states.

In many respects, although it has already moved beyond the minimalist form which would be favoured by economic liberals on many issues, the European Community continues to look more like an intergovernmental arena for bargaining between states, rather than a supranational arrangement which is likely to supersede them in the near future. It is this which makes debates over the distribution of the regional and social funds so sharp, as each member state tries to ensure that it does not lose out to another. Although the regional policies of individual states have to be maintained in line with those of the European Community, there is little evidence that European regional policies have cut across those of national governments. On the contrary European funds have largely been drawn on as reinforcement for those policies. Bargaining at European level has ensured that national governments have retained control over the direction of distribution. Since any bids for a share in the relevant funds have to be passed through the central authorities of member states, not surprisingly those states generally keep control over them. In principle — and usually in practice — every major funding proposal has to pass through the departments of central government.

And yet in some ways, this rather sceptical analysis seems to miss the point, too. It may be accurate enough as far as it goes, but it does not take into account the extent to which even negotiations of this sort already represent a substantial change in political practice. Such bargaining suggests a significant shift, because it implies the need for a process of institutionalized compromise. Once schemes have been set up — for educational collaboration or technological innovation, for example — they begin to develop a life of their own. A great deal of negotiation effectively takes place not between politicians of the different states, but between civil servants of those states and those of the European Commission.

Sometimes politicians react against the detailed decisions apparently made on their behalf. For example, in 1989 Kenneth Baker, the Secretary of State for Education withdrew from a European scheme (Lingua) which was intended to encourage the teaching of European Community languages throughout the member states. He did so on two grounds: firstly, that such schemes were not part of the purpose of the Community, which he claimed was principally economic; and secondly, because it might imply a commitment to the teaching of Community languages when the UK's own educational priorities might be different. The point of this example is not that it was particularly important in itself, but rather that it was the tip of a much bigger iceberg. This was one occasion on which a decision was taken to note what had been agreed and was about to be implemented, and to resist it. On a wide range of issues this process continues quietly without much resistance or even attention being drawn to it. The very existence of the European Commission means that many decisions are being made in an endless series of apparently mundane and relatively minor bargains struck between officials. Yet, the accumulation of these decisions may help to change the direction of policy without national governments having much control over it.

──────────────── ACTIVITY 6 ────────────────

How helpful do you think the three approaches outlined earlier are in explaining the developments discussed in this section? Remind yourself of their main features by looking back at the summary to Section 4.1. Try to identify briefly what each would predict and set it against what seems to have happened in the key areas in which they make predictions.

	Prediction	Outturn
Liberal market approaches		
Institutional approaches		
Marxist approaches		

It seems to me that undertaking this exercise confirms that if any of these perspectives is to be useful to us, then they need to be substantially modified. The first — liberal — approach tends to underestimate the pressures towards increased political integration within Europe. It is not so easy to de-couple the economic and political changes associated with the development of a single European market. But it continues to be an important theoretical tradition because of the critical attention it directs towards dangers of bureaucratization within European institutions. Its support of the market encourages scepticism about the claims made for political integration by those most likely to benefit.

The second — institutional — approach seems to be more helpful, but, in contrast to the liberal approach, it seems to be too eager to accept that economic integration will lead to political integration. The European Community has been far more successful in achieving the former than in moving towards the latter. Its member states continue to develop significantly different policies even in policy areas closest to the concerns of the Community, for example, relating to their national economics. There has been a bigger growth in inter-governmental bargaining (between officials) than in supranational decision making. Only if this approach begins to accept these weaknesses and to iden-tify a higher degree of separation between economy and politics will it be helpful. Marquand suggests that if further progress is to be made towards political (or, indeed, economic) integration then more explicitly political initia-tives are required, strengthening the role of the European Parliament and moving deliberately towards what he describes as 'federalism, or at least pre-federalism' (Marquand, 1989, p.219).

The marxist approach, as we have outlined it above, is also weak in explaining changes at the European level. If one believes that globalization has created an identifiably European set of capitalist enterprises, then moves to federalism and a new European state, have been very slow. If, on the other hand, one is less certain about the direction and extent of economic restructuring (as we were in Section 4.1), then changes at the political level have been far more extensive than one might have expected from looking at economic organiza-tions.

It appears that some state features are developing even before the predicted internationalization of capital. That process may be taking place, but, if so, it is as much the result of changes at the political level as a cause of them. And some marxists have begun to argue for a new 'Europeanism' as a way more effec-tively to reorganize economy and society to face the 1990s. Palmer maintains that if it is to survive 'Europe must become the citizens' Europe, the workers' Europe, the Europe of all those social constituencies currently excluded from or marginalized by existing power structures' (Palmer, 1988, p.190). He turns the marxist perspective on its head, arguing instead that the first steps may have to be the utilization and transformation of Europe's institutions in ways which will make it possible to resolve Europe's underlying economic problems and break away from the dominance of the USA.

Despite their weaknesses, then, all three approaches seem to be able to modify their initial starting points in ways which mean that each is still in contention as a possible interpretation of the rapidly changing politics of the European Community.

––––––––––––––––––––––––––––– ACTIVITY 7 –––––––––––––––––––––––––––––

What are the main elements which give the European Community suprana-tional rather than intergovernmental features?

I would identify three. First, some of the decisions of the Community are binding on its members, and the areas in which this is true are expanding. Second, it is increasingly being used as a forum through which a 'European' view is expressed on a number of issues. Third, its institutions are developing a life of their own, setting up processes of negotiation in ways which cut across national boundaries. But, remember in many areas intergovernmental negotiation remains important and member states retain a high degree of autonomy.

SUMMARY

- The strongest aspects of the EC are probably its economic (common market) ones, but this has not led to significant restructuring to produce strong European companies.

- There has been a growth of European political institutions in ways which imply that the EC is a supranational rather than an intergovernmental institution.

- Much of the activity of the EC is conducted through bargaining between senior politicans but there are also signs that practical decision making is being made at other levels on a day to day basis.

- None of the three approaches identified is adequate as a means of analysing the EC and its development. But each is open to modification which may make it more helpful.

A EUROPE OF THE 'REGIONS' AND 'LOCALITIES'?

The previous section considered arguments about the development of the European Community as a supranational political form. Our conclusions were relatively modest, but suggest that changes are taking place which are reducing the independent power of nation-states within it. In this section, I shall turn towards the subnational level to ask whether linkages are developing within the European Community which cut across the jurisdictions of its member states.

Formally the European Community is an organization of nation-states. But the very existence of a new set of European institutions may help to undermine those formal rules. The global system within which the game of politics is played has been transformed. Some hope that a new sense of Europe may be developed, based around regional rather than state consciousness, with the European Community becoming an alternative focus of attention, for regions, localities and the UK's component nations. The European Regional Development and Social Funds have already become direct areas of interest for local government and regional agencies (these funds and their operation are discussed in more detail in TV13). Informally, at any rate, links are being developed between local and regional agencies (including the development agencies) and European agencies, and the EC itself is committed to the development of what it calls a Europe of the regions, despite its current position within a Europe of nation-states.

The increased involvement of councils with various European Community (EC) schemes is one example of this. Within the UK, the driving force for taking up European Regional Development Fund (ERDF), European Social Fund (ESF), and targetted technology schemes — such as ESPRIT (European Strategic Programme for Research and Development in Information Technology) — comes from local and regional agencies (including enterprise boards and development agencies, where they exist). The departments of central government act either as enabling organizations, coordinating proposals, or, sometimes, as obstacles, but they are not usually the active initiators. Formally, any bids have to be transmitted through Whitehall, the Welsh, Scottish or Northern Ireland Offices but there can be little doubt that many local authorities play a major part in developing these initiatives.

The absence of a nationally sponsored regional policy in the UK of the 1980s, encouraged other groups — particularly local authorities — to try to develop their own, in relation to the European Community. As TV13 illustrates, with the case of Sheffield, such strategies may also be developed on a local rather than a regional basis.

A great deal of emphasis in the self help literature of local economic development puts a stress on EC schemes and how to gain access to them, and some of the most impressive (as well as most 'glossy') literature is oriented towards persuading EC agencies of the appropriateness of providing assistance to local schemes and drawing the attention of local agencies and enterprises to the value of making bids for European Community support. The case prepared by Lancashire Enterprises Limited and others, including Wigan Metropolitan Borough Council, Lancashire County Council and six other borough councils in the mid 1980s, as an Article 24 submission to the ERDF for support in redeveloping the Leeds and Liverpool Canal Corridor is a good example of the highly professional, well argued cases which have been put together. The initial submission moves from a summary of socio-economic indicators, showing the extent of the problem, towards an outline of the positive potential of development and a statement of costings and other sources of finance for the preparation of a 10 year Economic Development Plan. The package includes a

commitment to spending from all the authorities involved, which highlights the growing need for councils to work together on a more regional scale if they are to operate effectively in this sphere.

Although many member states (and particularly the UK) seek to retain a hierarchical model of decision making within the EC (like that represented in Fig 5a), there are pressures both from below (in the form of local authorities) and from above (in the form of the European Commission) to move towards a more 'triangular' form of negotiation (like that represented in Fig. 5b). Governments, including that of the UK, are afraid that such a shift might herald the possibility of direct Community involvement in the development of domestic policy.

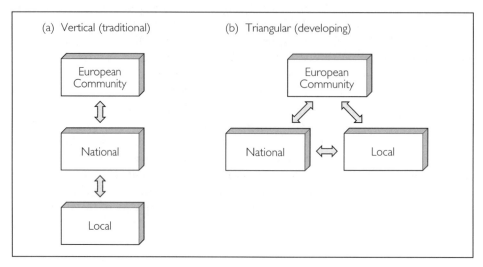

Figure 5   Inter-level Relations within the European regional and social funds
(Source: Mawson and Gibney, 1986)

The direction being taken by the European Commission in the distribution of its structural funds — that is those intended to achieve an economic restructuring in areas of high unemployment or low basic development, particularly the ERDF and ESF — may be encouraging a process of political restructuring, too. At the start of the 1990s these funds were distributed through regional partnerships — called Integrated Development Operations — which brought together the regional departments of government, local authorities and representatives of business. One of these was set up in the South Yorkshire and Humberside region, including Sheffield, and is discussed in TV13. Another early scheme was set up in the Strathclyde region in Scotland. Within these programmes, a broad framework is agreed with the European Commission, which retains a monitoring role on the eligibility of particular schemes for European funding, but in practice decisions on the allocation of funds are made by this regionally based committee. Committees of this sort seem to represent the beginnings of a move away from the vertical structure favoured by national government towards more triangular forms of hierarchy. But it is important to remember that even such committees still come under the leadership of departments of central government.

──────────────── ACTIVITY 8 ────────────────

It is possible to look at the hesitant moves towards a Europe of the 'regions' and 'localities' in terms of the three approaches outlined earlier (in Section 4.1). How do you think the changes would be interpreted within each set of approaches?

Liberal market approaches	
Institutional approaches	
Marxist approaches	

I suspect that supporters of the liberal market approach would take a fairly pragmatic view of developments. They would stress the ways in which they supported (or undermined) the position of the market, and would be highly critical if they felt regional or local initiatives interfered with its operation. They would tend to play down the political aspects of the new structures, emphasizing the continued importance of departments of central government, unless they were concerned that they were beginning to undermine national sovereignty or were encouraging the growth of European or regional bureacracies. The institutional approach, on the other hand, which is probably closest to the view which would be supported by senior officials of the European Commission (such as Bruce Millan, the European Commissioner responsible for regional policy, who is interviewed in TV13), would see the changes as providing examples of the way in which European politics is being restructured in the wake of increasing economic integration. For them, the new structures can be seen as the embryonic institutions of a new Europe, expressions of a Europe of the regions. Finally, the marxist approach would explain localization and regionalization as a consequence of the internationalization of capital, which breaks links at the level of the nation-state and increases the significance of the European level. But at the same time, the break up of the traditional nationally based/regionally dominant industries may increase the importance of the regional and local levels as sites for negotiaton between state and industry.

SUMMARY

- Direct links are being developed between the EC and local councils on a range of economic issues.

- There are also some pressures towards the development of regional forms of cooperation to take advantage of the structures and requirements of EC schemes.

- There are some signs that new regional institutions are being developed but largely on the basis of partnership arrangements between local institutions.

- Despite resistance from central government, new models are developing which move away from the traditional hierarchies of the unitary state.

- The three approaches (liberal, institutionalist and marxist) would assess the changes differently.

4.3   A WIDER EUROPE

The European dimension cannot and should not be restricted to a discussion of the European Community. The development and growth of the Community is itself only one expression of moves beyond the level of the old states which make up Europe. It reflects a process of economic and political restructuring which is beginning to make national boundaries seem less relevant. Even if many multinational companies are still based in one country they increasingly operate across national boundaries, in terms of siting production and, some-times, even control functions. The truly transnational company may still be difficult to identify in large numbers, but it is beginning to be easier to see what such companies would look like. At the same time, it is becoming clearer that decisions made in one country increasingly affect life in other countries, in ways which even the boundaries of the European Community cannot contain.

One obvious example of this can be seen in environmental issues. There is growing evidence that forms of power generation developed in one country affect health and welfare in others. Air-borne pollution from fossil fuelled power stations in the UK have substantially damaged forests in Norway and Sweden through the production of acid rain. The radio-active fall out produced as a result of the Chernobyl disaster in the Ukraine in 1986 (when a nuclear plant exploded) was carried across Europe with dramatic consequences for some foodstuffs, livestock and human health. Not surprisingly, therefore, environmental campaigns have increasingly been directed towards a wider notion of Europe.

Similarly, defence-related issues have begun to be debated at a European level, rather than in terms of the policies of individual sovereign nations. In part, of course, this was recognized in the two great post-war alliances of NATO (North Atlantic Treaty Organization) and the Warsaw Pact, but their interests went beyond Europe, and the increasing realization, particularly after the early 1980s, that Central Europe was likely to be the war zone began to undermine the certainties of both alliances, as campaigns (and governments) in Eastern and Western Europe looked for ways of reducing tension and levels of arma-ments, particularly nuclear weapons. The fragmentation of the monoliths of Eastern Europe in the late 1980s and the 1990s seems to have encouraged the search for a wider European identity.

─────────────── ACTIVITY 9 ───────────────

Can you think of any other examples of problems which need to be tackled within a European context?

───

I think it's easiest to think of environmental problems, which are often shared across boundaries, in ways which mean the originating nations tend not to worry about the full consequences of actions within their own boundaries. So, for example, the River Rhine/Ruhr carries pollution down from West Germany's industrial areas to the Netherlands and the sea. Industrial wastes carried down the Vistula in Poland to the Baltic have helped to pollute that sea with major implications for all those nations with coastlines on it. Decisions taken by one state on the disposal of waste in the North Sea will affect fishing possibilities for many other nations, and may also help to pollute their coastlines. The highest levels of industrial pollution are to be found in the industrial belts of Eastern Germany and Poland (in Upper Silesia), but are transmitted much further afield by air.

Another, sometimes related, set of issues concerns transport networks and infrastructure. Decisions taken in one country can have major impacts elsewhere. The decision to build the Channel Tunnel, for example, and the links it provides between the UK and Europe are likely to encourage forms of growth in Northern France and Southern England which will reduce growth prospects in other parts of the EC, directly for ports in Belgium, for example, but also more indirectly for areas which are effectively excluded by geographical distance from this potential growth pole. To stay with the example, for a moment, the building of the Channel Tunnel is clearly a decision which developed out of the growth of Europe as an economic entity, but this means that its immediate environmental impact on local areas (e.g. in Kent) was not an issue to which much thought was given, at least until local campaigns drew it to the attention of the developers, government and British Rail. From a slightly different angle, the operation of the ERDF tends to encourage road building in the member states, because road construction is defined as infrastructural investment and may be assisted from the fund, whilst subsidies to public transport (e.g. to keep fares down) would be explicitly excluded.

─────────────── ACTIVITY 10 ───────────────

In TV13 M. Ernecq, who is responsible for economic planning in the French region of Nord-Pas de Calais, says that he expects the region (and Lille in particular) to be a vitally important crossroads for the Europe of the late 1990s. He expects major development to take place in the wake of the Channel Tunnel.

Can you think of any ways in which your own locality has been influenced or is likely to be influenced by factors arising from the UK's position within Europe? In particular

• is development being encouraged?

• is the area being marginalized?

Any local evidence (e.g. from newspapers) which you have about this could be added to your Resource File — if you are keeping one. It will help in building up a picture of your locality and its position within a wider system.

───

The European Community was initially set up in the context of a divided Europe, and its early ambitions were explicitly constructed on the assumption of superpower rivalry. It was a *Western* European institution, part of the economic defences against communism. It was also intended to provide an alternative orientation for the Federal Republic of Germany, reflecting the apparently permanent division of Germany into two states. In the 1990s, these certainties have been fundamentally undermined, as the states of Eastern and Central Europe have moved away from communism, introducing market economies and opening themselves up to investment from the West. Germany has been reunited and both parts will be within the European Community, and many of the other states of Eastern and Central Europe may join. The European Community will be transformed once more, in the context of dramatic changes within the global system.

It may be dangerous to exaggerate the extent of change. And to assume that it will unproblematically lead to closer relations between all of Europe's states. The unification of West and East Germany, for example, (the Federal and Democratic Republics) leaves open the question of what is likely to happen to those parts of pre-1939 Germany, which are now parts of Poland, Czechoslovakia, and even the Soviet Union. There seems ample scope for a revival of major territorial conflicts within the nations of Eastern and Central Europe as old ethnic and national rivalries open up. Indeed, at the start of the 1990s, conflicts between republics within the Soviet Union seemed as significant as any between already existing nation-states.

But it also seems to be the case that Europe is becoming accepted as a political concept which goes beyond an alliance of sovereign states reflected in the institution of the European Community. So far I have tended to use positive examples to illustrate this — a concern for the environment, a concern about the dangers of war, particularly nuclear war. But, it may in conclusion be appropriate to identify an aspect which may be considered less palatable. The definition of Europe which is being developed through the European Community, but also in the more utopian visions of a United Europe from the Atlantic to the Urals, is one of exclusion as well as inclusion. Within the European Community, there will be free movement of labour, but those excluded by it will only be allowed to enter on severely restricted terms. The creation of a European 'people' also implies the identification of 'non-Europeans', whose privileges will be restricted. Past experience suggests that this is likely to encourage the development of a class of migrant labour never able to achieve full status as Europeans and always reliant on the vagaries of demand for employment, liable to be shipped back to their non-European homes when not required, and ineligible for most welfare benefits in the countries within which they work.

SUMMARY

- Environmental, military and other issues cut across national boundaries within Europe, beyond the limits set by the European Community.

- The restructuring of European states as a result of the upheavals in Eastern and Central Europe in the late 1980s and early 1990s means that the EC, too, will have to change its role, possibly becoming a focal point for a more extensive European system of states.

- But there are more uncertain consequences of building a new Europe: it explicitly excludes those defined as non-European, and it may open up new areas of conflict, including some of the boundary questions which seemed to have been settled in the post-war period.

5   CONCLUSION

The possibilities for political action at local and regional level are shaped by constraints imposed by the global system within which they operate The context of European politics, for example, has changed significantly over the past two or three decades, in part because of the ways in which the European Community has grown and increased in importance. More recently, in the late 1980s and early 1990s, upheavals in Eastern and Central Europe have brought still more dramatic change. But developments which take place at local and regional level may also serve to shape that system. A new Europe — and a new 'UK' within it — will be created as much by the actions of agencies operating at local and regional levels as it is by the actions of the European Commission or the European Parliament, or even by the actions of the leaderships of the EC's member states.

By this time, we have come quite a long way from the rather easy assumptions about the unitary state with which we started. Not only are there major differences between the politics of different local areas, but these are reflected in a variety of political practices of local authorities, and within regions and the national components of the UK. Now we have come to a point where, on some projections at least, it looks as if the UK state may disintegrate before our very eyes as links are made between councils and the European Community which completely bypass Whitehall and point towards the possibility of the united federation dreamed of by Churchill. It is perhaps time to call a halt and counsel caution. There certainly are signs that the unity of the UK is more fragmented at local level than many of the assumptions of the formal political system would suggest. And that Europe is becoming a more significant element in the decisions which affect our lives. I hope that you have been persuaded that it is important to look rather more closely at both local and European levels if we are to understand the meaning of national politics.

But the UK state survives and remains powerful. Some would argue that it became more centralized through the 1980s. All we are identifying here is a tendency, as yet barely developed, and in the context of the continued dominance and power of central UK based institutions. The likely conclusion of developments set in train by fragmentation within the UK and the development of new institutions is not yet by any means clear, even if some of the tensions already are.

Finally, let me turn to some of the key issues of the block. Understanding the local-global theme means acknowledging that we do not have to choose between localization and globalization. On the contrary, the two processes develop alongside and interact with each other. Each creates possibilities as well as tensions for the other. Even if we accept that global changes substantially limit what can take place at local level, it is important to recognize that it is at local level that those changes are interpreted, reinterpreted and given shape, particularly in the process of political development. The units in this block have sought to show that there are substantial differences in terms of culture, economic growth and politics between places within the UK. But the differences do not matter only as evidence of fragmentation. They also need to be acknowledged if we are to be able to develop a more complex picture in which cross-cutting relationships between different levels help to construct the world in which we all live.

REFERENCES

Aldcroft, D.H. and Richardson, H.W. (1969) *The British Economy 1870-1939*, London, Macmillan.

Anderson, J. and Ricci, M., (eds) (1990) *Society and Social Science: A Reader*, Milton Keynes, The Open University (Course Reader).

Audit Commission, (1987) *The Management of London's Authorities: Preventing the Breakdown of Services*, Occasional Paper No.2, London, HMSO.

Bassett, K., Boddy, M., Harloe, M., and Lovering, J. (1990) 'Economic and social change in Swindon' in Anderson, J. and Ricci, M. (eds) *Society and Social Science: A Reader*.

Beynon, H., Hudson, L., Lewis, J., Sadler, D., and Townsend, A. (1990) 'Coming to terms with the future in Teeside' in Anderson, J. and Ricci, M. (eds) *Society and Social Science: A Reader*.

Chartered Institute of Public Finance and Accountancy (1987) *Local Government Comparative Statistics*, London, Chartered Institute of Public Finance and Accountancy.

Committee of Inquiry into the Conduct of Local Authority Business (1986) *The Conduct of Local Authority Business* (Widdicombe Report), Research Volume IV: Aspects of Local Democracy, Cmnd 9801, London, HMSO.

Crafts, N.,(1990) 'British economic growth in the long run' in Anderson, J. and Ricci, M. (eds) *Society and Social Science: A Reader*.

Crewe, I. (1985) 'Great Britain', in Crewe, I. and Denver, D.(eds) *Electoral Change in Western Democracies*, London, Croom Helm.

Cutler, T., Haslam, C., Williams, J. and Williams, K. (1989) *1992 - The Struggle for Europe*, Oxford, Berg.

Dearlove, J. and Saunders, P. (1984) *Introduction to British Politics*, Cambridge, Polity Press.

Department of the Environment/Welsh Office (1983) *Rates, Proposals for the Limitation and Reform of the Rating System*, Cmnd 9008, London, HMSO.

Galtung, J.C. (1973) *The European Community: a Superpower in the Making*, Oslo and London, Universiteitforlaget and Allen and Unwin.

Gilroy, P., (1987) *There ain't no Black in the Union Jack. The Cultural Politics of Race and Nation*, London, Hutchinson.

Gyford, J. (1986) 'Diversity, sectionalism and diversity', in *Committee of Inquiry into the Conduct of Local Authority Business*, Research Volume IV, Aspects of Local Democracy, pp.106-32. London, HMSO.

Johnston, R.J. (1986) 'A space for place (a place for space) in British psephology: a review of recent writings with especial reference to the General Election of 1983', *Environment and Planning* A, 18: 573-98.

Johnston, R.J., Pattie, C. and Allsopp, G. (1988) *A Dividing Nation: the Electoral Map of Great Britain, 1979-87*, Harlow, Longman.

Jones, G.W. and Stewart, J.D. (1983) *The Case for Local Government*, London, George Allen and Unwin.

Lewis, R., (1989) 'Bruges or Brussels?' *Economic Affairs*, 9, 6: 6-8.

Mandel, E. (1978) *Late Capitalism*, London, Verso.

Marquand, D., (1989) 'The irresistible tide of Europeanization', in Hall, S. and Jacques, M. (eds) *New Times. The Changing Face of Politics in the 1990s*. London, Lawrence Wishart.

Massey, D. (1984) *Spatial Divisions of Labour. Social Structures and the Geography of Production*, London, Macmillan.

Mawson, J. and Gibney, T. (1986) 'English and Welsh local government and the European Community', in Keating, M. and Jones, J. (eds) *Regions in the European Community*, Oxford, Clarendon Press.

Mills, L. and Young, K. (1986) 'Local authorities and economic development', in Hausner, V. (ed), *Critical Issues in Urban Economic Development*. Vol. 1, Oxford, Clarendon Press.

Newton, K. (1976) *Second City Politics. Democratic Processes and Decision-making in Birmingham*. Oxford, Clarendon Press.

Newton, K. and Karran, T., (1985) *The Politics of Local Expenditure*, London, Macmillan.

Palmer, J. (1988) *Europe without America? The Crisis in Atlantic Relations*, Oxford, Oxford University Press.

Price, V., (1988) *1992: Europe's Last Chance? From Common Market to Single Market*. Occasional Paper 81, London, Institute of Economic Affairs.

Robins, K., (1990) 'Global local times', in Anderson, J. and Ricci, M. (eds) *Society and Social Science: A Reader.*

Sampson, A. (1971) *The New Europeans*, London, Panther.

Solomos, J. (1989) *Race and Racism in Contemporary Britain*, London, Macmillan.

STUDY SKILLS SECTION: HOW ARE YOU PROGRESSING?

Prepared for the Course Team by Kay Pole

This may seem an odd question now, just before the last unit of Block VI, and at a time when you may have already been to summer school. However, a quick glance back over the past months, and a look at the collection of blocks and units on your shelves, not to mention the notes and essays you've produced yourself, will show you how far you have come. You have done five or six essays and, while it may still seem as difficult to produce them now as it did in February, you will be getting better with practice. The essays themselves are probably getting longer; your problem now may be to cut them down to the required size because you have so much to say. You may also have been contributing to the discussion in tutorials — and didn't that seem daunting when you first went along?

In addition to all that, your summer school experience, whether it is over for you or yet to come, should consolidate what you are doing at home. If you haven't been able, or are not likely, to go to the D103 summer school, the excusal pack contains most of the learning activities you would have experienced there. Unfortunately we could not reproduce the social atmosphere of a real summer school — distance education can only do so much — but nevertheless working through the pack should give you a fresh perspective on the course and on your own progress, and a new determination to finish the course with colours flying.

So this is a very good time to sit back and take a deep breath, just as you are about to begin the run up to the end of the course, and the final six or seven weeks before the examination. We hope that you will have had a chance to attempt an examination question under exam conditions, either at summer school or if your tutor arranges such a session when tutorials resume. Most students find that, even when they feel convinced they haven't performed well in an exam (and that everyone else has done brilliantly, of course), the effort of taking it is fully justified. If possible take some time to practice answering questions in a set time — it's amazing how short forty-five minutes can seem. In addition, such an exercise can help you to organize your own revision before the examination, though it is also a good idea to attend any group revision sessions. Again these are generally available at summer school, or your tutor may arrange some.

THE GOOD STUDY GUIDE

It will also be worth your while to spend an hour or so reading the first two sections of Chapter 7 of *The Good Study Guide*. This is what we suggest you do at this point. By now you will be familiar with the book and its style and hopefully will be moving in and out of it with ease. The two sections we are recommending discuss the reasons for exams, and they cut through some of the myths about them.

ACKNOWLEDGEMENTS

Grateful acknowledgement is made to the following sources for permission to reproduce material in this unit:

Figures:

Figure 1: p.109. Newton, K. 'Birmingham and the national swing', *Second City Politics, Democratic Processes in Decision Making in Birmingham'*, © (1976), Reproduced by permission of the Oxford University Press. Figure 4: p.117. 'Differences from national average', *Local Government Corporative Statistics*, The Chartered Institute of Public Finance and Accountancy, (1987). Figure 5: p.130. Mawson J. and Gibney, T. 'Inter-level relations within the European regional and social funds'. *Regions in the European Community*, ed: Keating, M. and Jones, J., © (1986), Reproduced by permission of the Oxford University Press.

Illustrations

p.129: 'Eurocash' and 'What Next?', Sheffield City Council Information Department.

UNIT 26 CHOOSING BETWEEN EXPLANATIONS

Prepared for the Course Team by John Allen

CONTENTS

1   INTRODUCTION

As you know, these end units have a different focus from the rest of the block that you have just studied. As well as reviewing the arguments and ideas of the block, they also have the task of examining some of the key aspects of social science thinking. Each of these units has picked up and developed one or two aspects of how social scientists go about their work, how they actually 'do' social science. In Unit 9, one of the earlier end units, this activity was referred to as a process or cycle of enquiry, with distinct phases. You are now within sight of the end of that cycle, having worked through a number of the ways in which social scientists build an understanding of how society is put together and how it changes. Your attention has also been drawn to another kind of building work: how social scientists construct their explanations. From the start of the course, the importance attached to explaining, rather than simply describing, the world around us has been argued in virtually all of the end units. In fact, you already know quite a lot about how social explanations are put together and you should also have some idea of what a 'good' explanation looks like. The task of this unit is to strengthen that idea. In Section 4, you will be introduced to three ways in which it is possible to judge the 'success' of a theoretical explana- tion. This is the central purpose of this unit. When you have worked your way through the unit, I hope that you will feel confident about choosing between specific theories. Before we tackle the big issue of assessment however, we need to be clear about two things:

- What an explanation is
  and
- How we should compare explanations.

2   WHAT IS AN EXPLANATION?

This question has already been partially answered earlier in the course. Remember the point that was made in Units 4 and 9 about the need to go beyond description and classification if we wanted to say *why* something hap- pened? Although the point was made some time ago, its message is one that has appeared in all of the blocks. To explain something is to give an answer to a 'Why?' question. For example, Why does it appear easier for men to give up smoking than women? Why is there a growth in part-time work in today's economy? Why are some people rebellious and others cooperative in the same social situation? Why are some cities in slow decline while others grow rapidly? And so on. It was not enough merely to say when or where something happened or how long it took to happen, above all, we needed to know *why*? We needed to explain why things are as they are.

To explain why things happen, however, involves us in the kind of work that you have been doing in each of the review units. It involves the sifting and sorting of all kinds of evidence, the search for connections between the informa- tion available to us, the examination of existing arguments and ideas in the field, and a process of reasoning which moves us back from something that has happened towards the key aspects which explain it. In other words, it involves the cycle of social science enquiry: a process which is concerned with putting together an explanation of *why* things happen.

Knowing that we have to ask 'Why?' questions, however, does not tell us all we need to know about the nature of explanation. We also need to know what explanations actually *do* when they explain something and *what* it is that they explain. This may sound rather odd, to talk of explanations actually doing things, so let us separate the two points and take each in turn.

The 'Why?' question

In Unit 24 for example, each of the three explanations of regional inequality were concerned to establish the *cause* of that inequality. So it was argued that the major differences in fortune between the regions of the UK came about because of a shift in the supply and demand for capital and labour or because of the cumulative economic advantages conferred on some but not all regions, and so forth. The establishment of what *causes* something to come about then, is what these explanations were aiming to do, or rather it is what the type of explanations in Unit 24 were aiming to do. For there are explanations other than those which seek to establish the cause of something. Sometimes we may just want to know about the *purpose* or *role* of something, for example, the actual role of the state in managing the national economy, or we may just want to know about the *reasons* why some people draw their identity first and foremost from the fact that they regard themselves as 'English' and what this means to them. The first type of enquiry would lead us towards a functional mode of explanation, whereas the second would require us to combine under-standing with causal explanation. For our purposes, however, we need only note that there are different types of explanation within the social sciences. Here I wish to emphasize the fact that *all* explanations do more than describe or set the scene of events and that our concern in this unit is with those explanations that seek to identify the *cause* of why something happens.

Turning to the second point, the question of what explanations seek to explain, the answer to this may appear rather obvious. Explanations seek to explain what is going on and they do so by trying to make sense of the evidence available. This seems reasonable enough, although the 'logic' is not as straight-forward as some would have us believe. We learnt as much from Units 9 and 18. The facts you may recall, have no voice of their own. They cannot tell us whether our explanations are true or false, although the things that we see happening around us may force us to think again and perhaps to revise our line of argument. As new forms of evidence come to light they may persuade us to change our minds, although I suspect that initially we are likely to reflect upon the *reasoning* that led us to adopt a particular explanation rather than to switch immediately to another.

If, for example, I favoured a neoclassical explanation of regional inequality, yet the economic geography around me pointed in the direction of one or two regions continually benefitting at the expense of the rest of the country, I would probably question the coherence of my own reasoning before I took the more dramatic step of embracing the arguments of the cumulative causation school. The implication here is not that I would find the shift to a quite different explanation too disturbing or unsettling. On the contrary, my confidence in a neoclassical explanation and indeed its claims as to why regional inequalities come about would have been shaken. I would feel the need to look again at the various 'bits' of the neoclassical argument and to reassess their worthiness. For example, I would need to think again about the *clarity* of the concepts that a neoclassical account favours (markets, firms, individuals, competition, price signals, supply and demand) and the *coherence* of the reasoning that relies upon this bundle or network of concepts to establish the cause of regional inequality.

You already know from Unit 9 how important it is to work with precise definitions of concepts and the idea of concepts forming a bundle or network is an equally important issue that has been touched upon in previous theory-review end units. A *network of concepts* is at the core of any theoretical explanation. Whenever we bind a number of concepts into a network for the purpose of explaining something we are effectively putting theory together. In choosing to link the concept of markets to the concept of competition and in turn to the concepts of individual and choice, I am beginning to construct a network of concepts that tells us something about the nature of markets: that they are competitive and that we, as individuals, are able to express our preferences about say, where we live and work, and what we buy. We will look more closely at this particular example in Section 4.1, but for the moment, I want you to hold on to this idea of theories as comprising a network of concepts. For it is the choice of concepts and the way in which they are related to one another which generates a line of reasoning which, in turn, produces an explanation of *why* something happened.

SUMMARY

- To explain something involves more than giving a description of it; it involves asking *why* it happened, why certain events occured or why a particular state of affairs arose, and then trying to find out what *caused* it to happen.

- However, you should remember that within the social sciences there are different kinds of explanation and not all kinds are concerned to established causality.

- It is useful to think of theories as comprising a *network of concepts* which suggest certain connections between things which, in turn, help us to explain why something happened.

---

3   COMPARING EXPLANATIONS

It may seem rather peculiar here to raise the issue of comparison as something that we should consider. After all, we are at liberty to compare any range of explanations. The truth is, however, that not all comparisons are equally worthwhile. To ensure that the act of comparison is worthwhile we would need to be certain that we have in front of us explanations of the same thing, the same subject matter. Too often debates within the social sciences are conducted between positions that are actually attempting to explain different things or attempting to explain different aspects of the same thing. You may remember that this was just the sort of issue with which Unit 22 attempted to grapple in its concluding section. Is it really valid to compare Freud's psychoanalytic account of identity and interaction with, say, a biological explanation of identity and interaction? Even though they are talking about the same things, are they *really* attempting to explain the same aspects of human behaviour? Now *if* they are (and I stress if), then it is perfectly reasonable to place them side by side and to conduct some form of assessment of their 'success' as competing explanations. However if they are not seeking to explain the same things, then the exercise may tell us little about what each explanation has to offer in its own right. We can put this line of argument more forcefully:

Two or more explanations are comparable if they are attempting to explain the same thing or the same aspect of something. This is what we mean by *competing explanations*.

Let us take a closer look at what is involved in this view. I want to run through two examples which are based loosely on TV12, *Regions Apart*.

―――――― ACTIVITY 1 ――――――

The two statements which follow are concerned with the recent growth of Japanese inward manufacturing investment in the UK and why this has come about. I want you to read them now and decide which of the two statements you think involves explanations which compare *like with like*. Remind yourself of the point I made above before you read on.

EXAMPLE (A)

The first explanation of Japanese inward investment chooses to stress the broad 'global' context: the heightened nature of global competition in the 1980s and early 1990s, the emergence of Japan as a major power in the world economy, the strength of the yen and the weakness of the pound sterling, and so forth. In contrast, a second explanation chooses to emphasize the 'local' factors involved : the cheap cost of labour in the UK relative to other major European countries, EC tarriff barriers, the significance of English as the second language of the Japanese, and so on.

EXAMPLE (B)

The first explanation in this account addresses the arrival of two Japanese car manufacturers in the UK, Honda in Swindon and Toyota in Derbyshire, and attributes their actions to a combination of restrictive European car markets, the availability and price of semi-skilled labour in the two locations, the strength of the Japanese yen, the economic dominance of Japan in the world economy, as well as the fact that English is a foreign language familiar to the Japanese. The second explanation addresses the same set of events and the same actions. It speaks of the unstated codes and conventions of Japanese culture, the taken-for-granted assumptions of group behaviour among Japanese management teams, and the unconscious dispositions evident in the Japanese way of 'doing things'. It asks questions which seek to show cultural and socio-psychological differences between the British and the Japanese.

What conclusions did you draw? Does either example provide explanations that are attempting to explain the same thing or, even better, asking the same question?

In my view, example (a) meets this standard whereas example (b) does not. In example (a), even though the two explanations are focusing on different aspects of the possible causes of inward investment (one on the local dimension, the other on the global), they are asking the same question: Why are the Japanese investing in the UK? In this sense, they are rival explanations and thus directly comparable.

In example (b), each account wishes to explain a different aspect of Japanese behaviour. One is attempting to explain why Japanese multinationals invest in the UK and the other is trying to piece together the way in which Japanese socio-psychological make-up differs from that of the British. In short, the things to be explained are different and so too is what they wish to know about them. Thus they are complementary rather than rival explanations and in my view it would be far better to find out what each has to offer, rather than to set them side-by-side with some kind of evaluation in mind.

Another angle on the issue of comparison is to take the further example of two explanations of Japanese investment in the UK which, in this case, adopt different *methods* of study. Look at example (b) again, but this time assume that both explanations really are attempting to explain the *same* aspect of Japanese behaviour. However, whereas the first explanation produces a range of statistics to support its argument about why Japanese firms have invested in this country, the second explanation prefers to rely upon interviews with Japanese company directors and Japanese politicians to support its argument. Are the two explanations comparable in this instance?

In my view they are, simply because they share the same focus and wish to explain the same thing, even although they may have used different methods to reach their conclusions. The use of different methods does not limit the value of comparing the two explanations nor does it deny that they are in competition with one another.

Incidentally, this does not hold good for theories which couch their explanations at different *levels* of generality. Remember the different levels of theory that you were introduced to in Unit 18? It spoke, first, of grand theories, the broad traditions of thought that inform and influence our understanding of how society is organized and how it works. It spoke also of theories with a more specific focus, those which are rooted in one or other of the social science disciplines — in fact, the kind of theory we are interested in here, in this block.

Japanese investment in the UK

For example, there are economic explanations of the changing nature of work in society or the role of markets in the UK economy, and there are also political theories concerned to say something about the distribution of power in society or the significance of opinion polls or the meaning of certain patterns of voting behaviour. At this level, the *questions* asked by specific theories are about a particular aspect of society rather than about society as a whole. Finally, Unit 18 also referred to hypotheses which are perhaps best understood as one strand of specific theories. The significance of the differences between the levels was rehearsed in that unit and all that needs to be said here is that the different levels should not be collapsed by comparing, for example, marxism as a tradition of thought with say, a specific theory such as a neoclassical account of price movements or a pluralist account of pressure groups. There is little to be gained by comparing contrasting theories that are pitched at different levels of generality. Clearly they do not 'talk' to each other and therefore they are not in direct competition.

So one of the key aspects that you should take with you into the next section is that only certain sorts of explanation are worth comparing. We can compare and thus evaluate specific theories if broadly, they are attempting to explain the same thing. Competing theories, in this sense, are in some kind of dialogue with one another over which explanation is more 'successful' at answering the 'Why?' questions.

SUMMARY

- Explanations are in competition with one another if they are attempting to explain the same thing.

- It is also useful to remember that the use of different methods does not automatically rule out a comparison between explanations of the same thing, whereas different levels of theory will limit the value of comparison.

---

4   ASSESSING EXPLANATIONS

Now we know what an explanation is, and we also know that certain explanations are in competition with one another: those that explain the same thing, the same set of events or state of affairs. How do we choose between these conflicting explanations? Well, it is not enough to fall back on one's cherished beliefs and values. We should not judge a theory as more successful than another simply because we have a 'good feeling' about it. The whole idea of 'competing' explanations means that we should be considering ideas and arguments that may not agree with our own. It means weighing up all the evidence and the different points of view. More than that, it means saying why you find one explanation of say, political developments in Eastern Europe, better than another — more powerful in its arguments, more comprehensive in its reach, and more open in its ability to handle the pace of change in the world.

It is precisely these considerations that concern us in Section 4. If we have to choose between competing explanations, then we need some guidelines in order to make that choice. In a moment we will look at the first of these guidelines, the *explanatory power* of theories, but first of all I want to remind you of the discussions about this guideline which came earlier in the course. You may recall that in Unit 9 great play was made of the notion of the explanatory power of concepts and how this slid over into talking about the explanatory power of theories. And in Unit 18 the latter was taken a step further through an examination of how adequately theories were able to make sense of the available evidence — and how they lost credibility if they were only able to explain away exceptions. It is these kinds of issues that we shall pursue in Section 4.1. Following that, in Section 4.2, we shall look at the *explanatory reach* of theories. This guideline, it should be noted, refers as much to what a theory leaves out of an explanation as it does to the range and depth of its coverage. Finally, in Section 4.3 we will consider the *explanatory openness* of theories, that is, how well theories adapt and respond to the changing character of society and how reflective they are about the limits of what they can say.

As noted in the Introduction, we will draw upon arguments and explanations in the earlier units of this block to illustrate the three guidelines and, more generally, to review the subject matter of the block.

4.1   EXPLANATORY POWER

We frequently say things like 'that was a powerful argument' and 'that theory stood up well to the evidence'. Would either of these descriptions fit the three explanations of regional inequality that you met in Unit 24? Did the neoclassical account move compellingly from what it took as the cause of regional inequality to a demonstration of why this should be so and how well it meshed with the geographical evidence? Were you persuaded by the power of its reasoning? Or did you prefer the coherence of the marxist account and the way in which it traced the links back from a north-south divide to the very heart of the capitalist system itself? Whatever your thoughts, these are the sorts of questions that reveal the explanatory power of a theory. It is this emphasis upon how an explanation is put together; that is, its ability to *reason* why something happened the way that it did, because of the shifts in the supply and demand for capital and labour, or because of cumulative growth, or because of industry's relentless search for profitable returns, that concerns us here. We can draw out this process of reasoning in two ways. One concerns the *coherence* of the reasoning and the other concerns the *interpretation* of the evidence that flows from the reasoning.

IS THE REASONING COHERENT?

On the face of it, this question is asking whether or not any of the three explanations of regional inequality — neoclassical, cumulative causation, and marxist — actually work. In short, do they provide a step by step account of the changes in regional fortunes that actually holds together? If so, then what does this coherence look like? Remember the point that was made about theoretical explanations at the end of Section 2: that they comprise a network of concepts which generate a line of reasoning, which in turn tell us why something happened? Well it is the ways in which the key concepts of a theory are bound together, how they draw their meaning from one another, that gives a theory its coherence, part of its explanatory power. If we compare the marxist account of regional change with the neoclassical explanation we can obtain a better sense of how such explanatory networks are put together and how they set up a *causal* chain of reasoning which suggests why regional inequalities come about.

Central to the marxist argument is the claim that changes in the UK's geography cannot be understood unless we see those changes as part and parcel of the way in which the capitalist system works. There is an assumption in play here which suggests that the capitalist nature of the UK economy is something that we need to explicitly recognize before we address actual geographical divides, such as the north-south divide or the dominance of the south-east economy.

And as Unit 18 reminded us, such a recognition also involves an acceptance of other conceptual baggage. In choosing to open up the question of regional inequalities at the level of capitalism as a whole, marxists draw our attention to the key features of that system — as they conceive it. For our purposes, it is sufficient to note two central features: the class character of capitalism and the organization of production for profit. These features occupy a prominent position within the marxist framework and, more importantly for our concern here, they suggest the *direction* that an explanation of regional inequalities may well take.

For example, the priority accorded by marxists to the concepts of class, capital, and production, and the relationships that define them, leads them to consider the changing nature of work in the production process and hence the division of labour. They want to know whether or not tasks at work are becoming more deskilled or reskilled, and what if any are the implications of such changes for the number and range of jobs in different industries? Will changes in the nature of work reduce the size of the manual working class and stretch the middle classes? Why have the tasks of management and control seemingly become more important in manufacturing industry? As the questions addressed in Unit 24 are of a geographical kind, the analysis is naturally extended to an understanding of how the division of labour is structured over space to satisfy the profitable requirements of industry. As new industries emerge and new ways of organizing production and work come to the fore, so, in turn, industries and firms are seen to reorganize their production over space. The argument that flows from this is that a new spatial division of labour, a new map of class relations, and hence a new pattern of regional inequality have emerged. Figure 1 gives you an idea of the network of concepts that generates this line of reasoning.

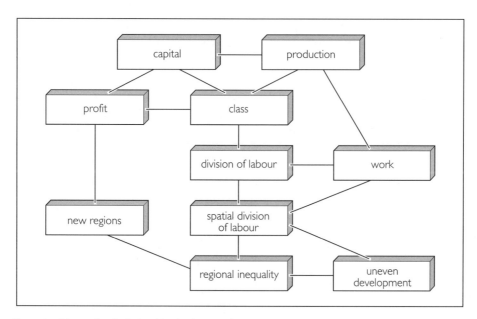

Figure 1   Network of relationships in the marxist argument

Representing a chain of reasoning as a network of relationships does tend, however, to give the impression that the whole process of putting together an explanation is rather simple and straightforward. You could even say that it looks like a logical exercise. In practice the construction of this model of relationships involves precisely the kind of work that I spoke of in Section 2: the sifting and sorting of the evidence, the search for connections among the evidence, the examination of existing explanations, including those within the marxist tradition, and the step by step reasoning that makes sense of it all. In the short statement such as the one above, 'the division of labour is structured over space to satisfy the profitable requirements of industry' all of the class and production relationships are presupposed yet unstated. In other words, the short statement only makes sense *because* of the network of concepts which underpin it; namely the interrelationships between capital, class, production, profit, spatial division of labour, and uneven development. As a bundle of concepts however, they suggest a possible explanation of regional change.

Does the explanation hold together? Do the steps in the argument lead compellingly from one to another? Well, it has a starting point which carries the causal weight of the explanation, namely the class character of capitalist production and the pursuit of profitable investments. But can we legitimately *infer* from this causal starting point the emphasis that the explanation places upon *particular* aspects of the economy, such as work and the division of labour, and the *connections* that it draws between changing class relations, capital investment, and a new geography of inequality? Is it really the case that a coherent line of explanation can be constructed which moves from an abstract proposition that class divisions in a capitalist economy are based on the ownership and control of production to a more specific proposition about the nature of regional inequality and uneven development? If each step in the argument is closely linked to the one before and you are quite sure that there are no 'jumps' in the reasoning, then the explanation is coherent. Any gaps however in the line of reasoning, any concepts in the network that appear vague or ill defined, are an indication that the explanation may be lacking in coherence.

For example, if the marxist account merely *asserted* that uneven development is the result of capitalism rather than demonstrating the links between cause and effect, then it would be fair to label such an account as incoherent. There is an observable leap in the reasoning from an abstract proposition to an alleged outcome. None of the connections have been drawn. Perhaps we can see this more clearly by setting up a comparison. If we judge the relative 'success' of two explanations (of regional inequality) we should be able to get a sharper sense of the idea of coherence.

In Unit 24 you will have noticed that the neoclassical account of uneven development had a different starting point from that of the marxist explanation and that it chose to focus upon different aspects of the economy according to the concepts that it favoured. It drew its starting point from a set of liberal

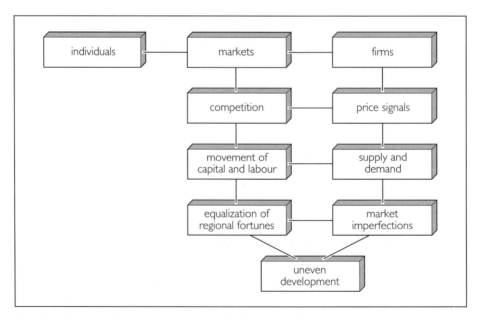

Figure 2   Network of relationships in the neoclassical approach

assumptions which gave centre stage to rational actors — in this case, firms and individuals — who were then seen to respond to price signals in a competitive market place. And in sharp contrast to the marxist explanation, the economy was regarded as a series of micro-relationships that are focused on the activities of markets and the mechanisms of supply and demand. As with the marxist account however, the concepts of markets, firms, individuals, competition, price signals, supply and demand form a *network of concepts* which draw their meaning from one another and, in turn, suggest certain *connections* between aspects of the economy and regional developments. For example, the importance neoclassicists attach to the mechanisms of supply and demand highlights the movement of capital and labour between rich and poor regions. As workers and employers respond to market price signals they seek to achieve the 'best' position for themselves in the regions. The anticipated result in this instance, as you know, is a shift towards the equalization of regional fortunes, even though the presence of market imperfections, such as inequalities in the housing market, will lessen that shift.

Can you pull out the causal chain in this explanation? While it is possible to construct a more complex version of the neoclassical argument (as it is for the marxist account), there is I think a clear progression in the reasoning of the neoclassical position. In outline the 'logic' looks something like this:

1 Individuals and employers are in a position to make rational choices about where they, respectively, choose to work and where they choose to invest.

2 Such choices will be made in the marketplace in response to the shifts in the supply of and demand for capital and labour between the regions.

3 Individuals and employers will attempt to achieve the 'best' position for themselves. People will migrate to jobs and firms will invest in plant and machinery in response to the 'price signals' which tell them where the best returns — wages or profits — are obtainable.

4 As competition between firms for labour in the 'south' pushes up wages, unemployed or low paid workers in the 'north' will move 'south' to take advantage of the higher wages. Equally, while cheaper labour costs are to be found in the 'north', together with lower rents and construction costs, firms will move north to seek better returns on their investment.

5 With individual workers moving in one direction across the country and capital investment moving in the other, there is a general tendency — over time — for regional fortunes to even out, despite the persistence of market imperfections.

Now what is at issue here is not whether you agree with this explanation of uneven development, but whether you find the steps of the argument convincing. Again, are there any 'jumps' in the chain of reasoning? Does the line of argument falter or does it move persuasively from cause to effect? As with the marxist account, I think that there is a certain elegance to the neoclassical argument. But the power of both explanations is not a product of their elegance, it is rather the coherence of their arguments that lends them credibility.

Which of the two is the more *powerful* at explaining uneven development? It is not possible to answer this question on the basis of coherence alone, as we have yet to assess how well the two explanations account for the changes happening 'out there'. However, you might like to spend a few minutes thinking about which of the two theories includes *more* of the causal chain that explains regional inequality. You may find it useful to include the cumulative causation school in your deliberations and to complete the following activity.

―――――――――――――――――――― ACTIVITY 2 ――――――――――――――――――

In this activity, I want you to explore how the cumulative causation explanation of regional inequality is put together. The activity will help you to recap the main points we have been considering in this section in respect of the neoclassical and the marxist accounts. It will also help you to assess the coherence of Myrdal's explanation.

1   What does Myrdal take to be the cause of regional inequality? The name of the school is an obvious indication, although you should think carefully about what exactly produces the cumulative effect.

2   Is there a causal chain supported by a network of concepts? The metaphors of 'core' or 'periphery', 'backwash', and 'spread' effects, and 'virtuous' and 'vicious' circles play an important part in the explanation. Do they exhaust the conceptual content of the model?

3   Are there any 'jumps' in the reasoning? In order to work this out you will have to establish the starting point of the explanation and then trace the argument step by step — much as we did with the neoclassical position.

IS THE EVIDENCE ACCOUNTED FOR?

So far, we have been trying to decide whether or not the three theories of regional inequality in Unit 24 possess a coherent explanation of the UK's changing geography. For the most part, however, we have managed to avoid talking about the evidence for change. We know a lot about what is said to be happening 'out there', but we know little about the *relationship* between theory and evidence in the three explanations. Does the available evidence support the respective claims of all three explanations? Or is one explanation better than the other two in accounting for the evidence?

As you know from Unit 18, there is no simple answer to such questions. There we saw that theories of the state can *escape* the facts, the theories can make sense of all different kinds of evidence, although that is not to say that we can simply make-up explanations. The theories of the state that we addressed and certainly the hypotheses they generated were also *vulnerable* to the facts. The same holds for theories of regional inequality. We can explore the two different aspects of the relationship between theory and evidence by looking at each in turn. After that we shall draw some initial conclusions about how we may choose between the three explanations of regional inequality.

The first aspect refers to the underdetermination of theories by the facts. Theories may *escape* the facts because the evidence cannot prove conclusively which theory is correct. The same piece of evidence, the same set of regional changes for example, can support different theories. Think of one of the examples given in Unit 24: the north-south divide. According to most neoclassical geographers the gap between north and south, as we know, is the result of market imperfections in the supply and demand for labour and investment capital which, over time, will even out as market forces reassert themselves. For most marxist geographers however, the north-south divide is the product of the different kinds of investment and the different kinds of jobs in the two parts of the country. The geographical divide reflects the ways in which capital 'uses' the regions and this will change over time as new industries seek out new profitable spaces. So the same piece of evidence can be interpreted in different ways without, it would seem, any loss of power to either theory.

Let me turn to the second aspect, the *vulnerability* of explanations to the facts. Does this enable us to judge which of the three is the better theory? Take the example of the UK's changing regional geography set out at the end of Unit 23.

It was reproduced in Unit 24 and there it was apparent that the neoclassical and the cumulative causation schools were pulling out different periods and different places to support their argument. (You may find it useful to flip back to the relevant sections in either Unit 23 or 24). While the neoclassical argument refers to a succession of regional economies taking the lead on the basis of major industries throughout the nineteenth and into the twentieth century, the cumulative causation school focuses upon the dominance of the City of London and the south east in the UK economy, especially in recent times. In one sense then both explanations 'fit' the facts — but at different times and in different places. Thus it is quite possible that the claims of both theories may be rather weak or uncertain in other periods and in other locations. If, for example, the south east were to break away from the rest of the UK to form one of Europe's 'core regions' in the 1990s (one of the scenarios etched at the end of Unit 24) then this evidence would challenge the central claims of the neoclassical argument and raise doubts about the power of that explanation.

The S.E. 'breaking away' to join Europe?

So what happens 'out there' can tell us something, the evidence is not entirely without a voice of its own. Changes that occur in society do require us to reflect upon the structure of our arguments and they can help us to choose between explanations. The key word here is *help* us to choose between explanations, because the evidence on its own does not enable us to judge the 'success' of a theory. We need to combine this aspect with an assessment of the coherence of an explanation. Together, the two aspects provide us with the means to judge the *power* of a theory, without falling back onto our cherished beliefs or hunches.

SUMMARY

The explanatory power of a theory is assessed along two dimensions

- The coherence of its reasoning; that is, whether each step in the overall argument is clearly linked to the one before so that a causal chain of reasoning is established.

- The interpretation of the evidence. This is a more difficult dimension to work with as theories may escape the facts. Having said that, forms of evidence, new or old, may constrain theories. You need to search out forms of evidence which look as if they will counter or weaken an argument.

Remember that an explanation may still be powerful even if you radically disagree with its main propositions. It is up to you to come up with *other* reasons for its inadequacy.

4.2   EXPLANATORY REACH

The explanatory reach of a theory is not concerned with how well an explanation is put together, but rather with its *empirical scope*. Now, you have met this term before in Unit 9, where the range of things 'covered' by a concept (periods of history, different societies, and so forth) referred to its empirical scope. Some concepts we were told are broad in scope, such as patriarchy, while others are more restricted in their coverage, such as the concept of the working class, which draws its meaning from the specific character of industrial societies. The same can be said of theories. Some theories cover broad sweeps of history, perhaps taking in large tracts of the globe on the way, while others are more concerned with regional or national events, over say, a brief yet critical time period. Whatever the empirical coverage of a theory however, its reach is not something that we can assess until we know what it is that it wishes to explain. Once we have an idea of the *questions* that a theory is asking, then we are in a position to assess what it misses out and whether the gaps are damaging or not.

EMPIRICAL SCOPE

We can piece together what is involved in the use of this guideline by looking at the different explanations of local social change laid out in Section 3.2 of Unit 23. The two types of explanation that I have chosen, one represented by the arguments of Harvey and Smith and the other by the work of Urry and Cooke, are in competition with one another over how and why local change comes about. They are both asking similar questions about the changing fortunes of regional or local areas and therefore it is possible to compare and assess their explanatory reach. As before, you may find it useful to have the relevant unit to hand as we contrast the two positions.

In comparing the coverage of the two approaches, one of the first things that struck me was the breadth of the statements in the position argued by Harvey and Smith. It was not that I found their statements to be woolly or vague; on the contrary they were crisp and to the point. Consider their main assertion, that the differences between regions is essentially the outcome of shifts in the character of the international capitalist economy. There is no mistaking here as to where they place the causal emphasis; it is at the international and national levels, as today, capital moves across the globe taking advantage of different regions in different ways. For Urry and Cooke however, it is precisely the breadth of this vision that limits the empirical scope of this type of explanation. The sorts of evidence that they consider, for example, the *specific* character of regions, their political complexion, their cultural form, and so forth, are absent from Harvey and Smith's account of local social change. And for Urry and Cooke, it is the local characteristics of places, their histories and their specificities, that play an important part in shaping the way in which a region relates to the international economy. For them, the local detail is as important as the global detail.

Now, in one sense, any explanation is incomplete. As events change the world around us, our theories are likely to be in need of revision. But this kind of theoretical dating is not the kind of incompleteness that concerns us here. Rather it is, as noted earlier, what has been left out of an account that may limit its 'success' as an explanation. So on this count, what assessment would you arrive at on the empirical scope of Harvey and Smith's position? Because their account neglects the local dimension, does that imply that it has a restricted explanatory reach? From Urry and Cooke's point of view, it would imply just that. They would argue that any explanation of changing regional fortunes which failed to consider *in depth* the character of regions lacks scope. It is not comprehensive. In reply, however, Harvey and Smith would very likely argue that in placing causal weight on the particularity of regions, Urry and Cooke have distorted the importance of the local dimension in their explanation of regional change. Note here, however, that we have slipped back to the *power* of an explanation at the expense of its empirical *reach*. If Harvey and Smith's position lacks empirical scope, emphasizing as it does global breadth rather than local depth, that does not imply that it is weak on explanatory power too. Their reasoning may be coherent, even if their scope is limited.

GEOGRAPHICAL SCALE

The reach of an explanation therefore should not be equated with its breadth of coverage. If that were true, then the 'best' theories would always be those with a global, historical dimension. This may be so in relation to some issues, but not as a general rule. Equally, I do not wish to suggest that a local as opposed to a global focus offers greater explanatory reach. Although I have stressed the more detailed local coverage of Urry and Cooke's approach, that does not mean that there is some kind of choice to be made between either a local or a global focus. Rather it is the *relationship* between the local and the global that is crucial, and how it is conceived.

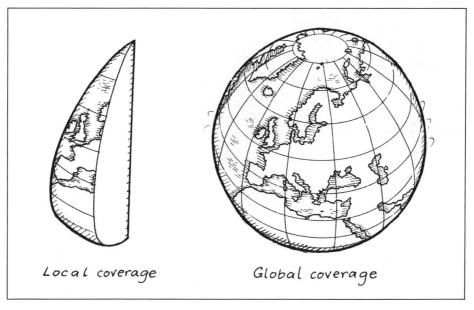

Local coverage   Global coverage

The 'biggest' theories aren't always the best theories

If we consider Harvey and Smith's position again, we see that it is a kind of 'top-down' argument, whereby the international capitalist economy shapes the fortunes of regional economies. The causal relationship between the local and the global is in this case, one way, from the global to the local. For Urry and Cooke however, the relationship between the local and the global is two way. International capitalism is indeed regarded as a causal factor behind the changing fortunes of regions, but not in isolation from the social and economic fabric of the regions themselves. The particularity of the regions shape their own destinies, although they do so within the context of wider global economic forces.

What is inevitably missing from this formulation however, is the precise way in which the local and the global *interact*. There is no 50 : 50 formulae; one that we can apply regardless of what it is that we wish to explain, whether it be a declining region or a growth region, a recent turn of events or a past state of affairs. In some instances the local level will carry the causal weight and in others the global level may well be more important in an explanation. The scale at which we pitch an explanation will depend upon precisely what it is that we set out to explain. Different questions or different issues will direct us to various sources of evidence.

Poll Tax riots

If, for example, we set out to explain the motives of those involved in say, an urban riot, then we may feel that we can collect all the evidence that we need from local sources — local grievances, local pressure groups, local institutions, and the like. Indeed, such sources may be perfectly adequate. On reflection however, we may feel that local sources are limited, merely hinting as they do at the spark which ignited the popular unrest and indicating the need to consider the event in a wider, national context. If the disturbance involved a clash between local people and the police, then we would also need to consider national policing policies and any recent state legislation relating to the event. For example, an explanation of the local disturbances around the Community Charge legislation in 1990 would require a national as well as a local focus.

Moreover, if we want to explain *why* popular unrest occurred in some towns and cities and not others, then we would very likely have to broaden the scope of our explanation to embrace the international level. I stress, very likely, because the case is not proven. However, if the areas of the country in which the riots occurred were among the poorest economically, we would have to assess the impact of global economic forces in and across those areas in order to build up an adequate explanation of local political conflict. The point that I wish to pull out of this sketch is that it is possible to have equally successful explanations that are pitched at a local, a regional, a national or even an international level. It depends, as stated earlier, entirely upon what it is that you set out to explain. In the sorts of things that we have looked at in this block, for example, the changing fortunes of regions and the shifting relations between local and national state, the scope of an explanation will include both the local and the global dimensions.

You will find that the following activity provides a useful recap of the main points in this section.

ACTIVITY 3

In turning back to Section 3.2. of Unit 23, you will have also come across a third explanation of local social change, one based upon the physical or environmental characteristics of a region. The explanation was a 'local' one, which drew heavily upon the 'natural' characteristics of an area (its resources, landscape, climate, etc.) to make sense of a region's economy and way of life.

Take another quick look at that section and compare the kinds of 'local' evidence selected with the sources identified by Urry and Cooke. Now decide which of the following statements are correct.

Urry and Cooke's position has *greater* explanatory reach because:

1   It has greater depth than an argument based solely on local environmental characteristics.

2   It was developed some time later.

3   It starts from the local and works its way up to the global.

Yes, you have guessed it. None of the statements are *quite* correct. Each of them points to a potential misunderstanding about the reach of an explanation. The first statement misses the point because it prioritizes depth over breadth. Urry and Cooke's approach considers regional change within the context of international economic change. It is not simply a 'local' social explanation concerned with the particularity of places.

The second statement conflates the timing of a theory with its strength. Certainly it is the case that successive approaches often act as correctives to the perceived weaknesses of earlier accounts. But the passage of time itself does not guarantee that the more recent account is stronger or better. The latest explanations are not necessarily the best explanations.

The third statement misrepresents Urry and Cooke's approach. If anything, their account of regional change has greater explanatory reach because they do attempt to connect the local to the global.

SUMMARY

The explanatory reach of a theory refers to the coverage of an explanation, its empirical scope. We can assess the coverage in two ways.

- By identifying what a theory leaves unexplained and then assessing whether or not the gaps weaken the explanation. In order to carry out this evaluation we need to know, first, what a theory seeks to explain.

- We also need to look at the pitch of an explanation and whether it is appropriate or not. There is no hard and fast line to this assessment, only a sense of what is appropriate. Should it be weighted to the local or to the global, for instance?

Remember that an explanation may have a limited explanatory reach, yet remain powerful in terms of its causal reasoning. A theory may be sound on one criterion, yet weak on another.

4.3   EXPLANATORY OPENNESS

The third guideline is of a rather different order from the first two, although no less important for that. It is different because it is concerned with the broad qualitative characteristics of a successful theory: its *adaptability* to the changes in the world around us, its *responsiveness* to criticism, and its *boundedness*, that is an awareness of the limits of what it can explain. Taken together, these three characteristics are what we mean when we refer to theories as 'open'. Such theories do not close off debates; indeed they keep debates moving and with it our ideas of what is happening around us. In many ways, such theories are the very 'lifeblood' of the social sciences in that they are likely to throw up new issues and pose new questions. To get a better sense of what we mean by 'open' however, we need to look at each of the three characteristics in turn.

ADAPTABILITY

There are at least two ways in which we can judge how well a theory is able to *adapt* to new things. One is the ability of a theory to adapt to new lines of research or the fact that we see things differently now, in a new light perhaps. Another is the ability of a theory to adapt to changed circumstances, new events or dramatic shifts in world affairs. There are examples in earlier units of the block which illustrate both aspects.

I should like to take as my first example the whole bundle of concerns that we now label as 'environmental issues' — the onset of global warming, the threat of climatic changes, the dangers of pollution, and so forth (if you have not already attended the D103 Summer School, these are some of the issues that you will explore in relation to the Block VI materials). There are lots of angles that we could pursue about the environment, but I want to take up one in relation to the issue of economic growth. Many of us now recognize that there are links between economic growth and the environment and that these links raise all sorts of questions about the type of growth that we want. It is probably fair to say that it has been environmentalists who have drawn our attention to the reasons why issues of economic growth (and for that matter regional economic growth) cannot be separated from their environmental costs. So, when we talk about regional growth strategies we also have to consider whether they include industries that are harmful to the environment and possibly to the workers within those industries. Indeed, some theorists would go further and would argue that by opening up the relationship between the environment and economic growth, we actually change the way in which *we think* about growth. Academic and political opinion is divided over this, but if it is the case then it implies that those economic geographers who remain closed to environmental issues will provide one-sided or deficient explanations of regional economic growth. Imagine, for example, a regional account of the coal industry that did *not* explore the tension between job growth and pollution. In this case it could be argued that the notion of growth is treated in such a shallow way that it fails to acknowledge the greater awareness today of environmental concerns, both locally and globally.

A Coal fired power station — a source of pollution

My second example is that of the creation of European economic institutions and thus the potential for a European identity and a distinctive European politics to become a reality. These developments were discussed in Unit 25 from a range of different theoretical positions. For me, one of the most interesting aspects of that discussion was the way in which the political theorists — from the liberals through to the marxists — were straining to make sense of the new developments. When all is said and done, is the European Community nothing more than a bargaining arena between nation-states? Or are we really seeing the development of a supranational rather than an intergovernmental agency? Or has the growth of European-based multinationals started a process which will end with a more integrated, federal Europe? Again, we cannot be sure, but we can get a sense of the open way in which the different theories are trying to adapt to, rather than close-off to, the fairly dramatic changes that have taken place in Europe. Although we do not have any answers yet, they are each seeking the *direction* of change in response to the shifting dynamic of Europe.

RESPONSIVENESS

The European Community also provides us with an insight into the sorts of things that a *responsive* theory would take on board. In Section 4.1 of Unit 25, we were told that the three explanations of contemporary change within the European Community could usefully be developed in various ways. The liberal explanation was challenged for not making explicit its criticisms of the EC as a bureaucratic obstacle to economic competition; the marxist approach was challenged for its neglect of politics as a force for change that is separate from wider economic developments, and so on. These challenges are rarely as combative as the language conveys and for the most part this 'talking' between theories is the sign of a responsive social science. In the course of debate, those involved will try to expose gaps in the coverage of other accounts whilst defending their own viewpoint. They may raise new questions and accuse others of substantial neglect (as we have seen in our discussion of explanatory reach). Such criticism may spur the theory being challenged to *respond* to and to take account of the alleged shortcomings. Now in one sense, we cannot and should not expect any one theory to 'explain everything', and so part of the dialogue between competing explanations will inevitably involve accusations of neglect and oversight. How theories react to and deal with such accusations however is an indication of their responsiveness.

BOUNDEDNESS

The *boundedness* of a theory can be judged by looking at how far a theory or theorist recognizes the limits of an explanation. From the way that explanations are set out, it is not always easy to see exactly where the boundaries are, but we do have one good indicator - the actual *claims* of a theory. For example, we know from Unit 25 that national and local state policies have played a significant role in reshaping local and regional economies. Indeed, politics enters into questions of regional growth and decline in such an integral way that it all seems rather surprising that the three explanations of regional inequality in Unit 24 hardly touch on the issue. Perhaps they should have been political economy explanations, but that really depends upon the nature of their claims — what they set out to explain. If all that they wanted to do was to give an economic explanation of regional change and uneven development in the UK, then that is fine. If, however, they remained silent about the impact of political policies upon the regions because they thought them unimportant, or they assumed some kind of priority of the economic over the political dimension of change, then they are guilty of attempting to explain too much on the basis of too few insights. In other words, they do not recognize how *partial* their accounts are.

As a brief aside, we should also note that different levels of theory are likely to be open in varying degrees. The grand theories, the traditions of thought, are not likely to be too disturbed by the appearance of new ideas or new pieces of evidence. Their hold in the arguments across the social sciences is a tenacious one, although we will have to wait until Unit 30, the last of these end units, to explore this aspect in greater detail. In this unit we have restricted our attention to the assessment of specific theories.

SUMMARY

The mark of an open theory is one that does not close off debates, but rather keeps them moving. We can assess this quality along three dimensions

- Adaptability to change — whether the change refers to new economic, social, or political circumstances or to new ways of thinking about familiar topics.

- Responsiveness to criticism — how far a theory is open to probing questions and new ideas (note the overlap with adaptability).

- Boundedness — how self-conscious a theory or theorist is about the limits of an explanation.

5 CONCLUSION

I have suggested that competing theories can be evaluated by considering their explanatory power, their explanatory reach, and their explanatory openness. These guidelines apply to specific theories that you have met in previous blocks as much as they do to the kinds of geographical explanations found in Block VI. They can be used to assess a range of explanations across the social sciences, although you should be sensitive to the differences between what is studied in say psychology from that of economics or politics.

At this stage, you should also be aware that none of the guidelines come with a guarantee which states that every time you use them you are assured of success. They can be used or misused, and we can never be entirely sure that the guidelines have been conclusively applied to a particular theoretical debate. And moreover, as we have stressed throughout in these theory-review end units, it is somewhat misleading to think that the real world out there will provide us with a simple or transparent proof of our explanations. I know that life would be easier for us all if it did, but the bottom line is that society does not disclose its workings to us directly, no matter how hard we may squint at it. This always leaves room for doubt. Doubt, for example, over how far our explanations do represent what actually happens in society and doubt over how far our accounts are shaped and influenced by the persuasive arguments put forward by others. In fact, the mark of a good theory is that it is *fallible*, that it can be challenged, and good social scientists recognize this by exposing their views to criticism — as well as being critical of others.

Having said that, the guidelines set down in this unit *do* provide you with the means to judge just how good or how bad a theory is. They should help you to recognize descriptions which call themselves 'explanations' and they should also help you to recognize complementary explanations which parade as 'rival' accounts. More than that, in Section 4, I hope that I have shown how it is possible to take an explanation apart, to look closely at how well it is put together and to see what it leaves unexplained. In D103 there are lots of theories that have something to offer, but that does not mean that all theories are equally successful. Unless you have some ideas about how to examine the strengths and weaknesses of theories you will be thrown back onto your values, your beliefs, about what is a good explanation and what is a poor explanation. Your hunch may well be right I grant you, but a hunch will not tell you why you are right or enable you to point out to others where they are wrong. The danger here is that your view on a topic will be just that — your view — and as good as any other. In studying D103 you have the means to say more than that.

ACKNOWLEDGEMENTS

Grateful acknowledgement is made to the following sources for permission to reproduce material in this unit:

Photographs
p.146: Network Images; *p156*: Melanie Friend/Format; *p.159*: Environmental Picture Library.

SUGGESTIONS FOR FURTHER READING

These readings are optional. They will not form part of the course assessment and we provide them purely for your interest — should you wish to pursue the topics and issues of this block further.

David Smith, *North and South: Britain's Economic, Social and Political Divide*, 1989, Harmondsworth, Penguin.

Kevin Morgan and Andrew Sayer, *Microcircuits of Capital: 'Sunrise' Industry and Uneven Development*, 1988, Cambridge, Polity.

John Palmer, *Europe Without America? The Crisis in Atlantic Relations, 1988*, Oxford, Oxford University Press.

Michael Harloe, Chris Pickvance and John Urry (eds.), *Place, Policy and Politics: Do Localities Matter?*, 1990, London, Unwin Hyman.